ROHITH VEMULA DOSSIER
My Birth is My Fatal Accident

Inspired by a real-life tragedy that sparked national outrage
AMITABH KUMAR

BLUEROSE PUBLISHERS
India | U.K.

Copyright © Amitabh Kumar 2025

All rights reserved by author. No part of this publication may be reproduced, stored in a retrieval system or transmitted in any form or by any means, electronic, mechanical, photocopying, recording or otherwise, without the prior permission of the author. Although every precaution has been taken to verify the accuracy of the information contained herein, the publisher assumes no responsibility for any errors or omissions. No liability is assumed for damages that may result from the use of information contained within.

BlueRose Publishers takes no responsibility for any damages, losses, or liabilities that may arise from the use or misuse of the information, products, or services provided in this publication.

For permissions requests or inquiries regarding this publication, please contact:

BLUEROSE PUBLISHERS
www.BlueRoseONE.com
info@bluerosepublishers.com
+91 8882 898 898
+4407342408967

ISBN: 978-93-7139-588-5

Cover design: Yash Singhal
Typesetting: Namrata Saini

First Edition: June 2025

Dedication

To Mrs Radhika Vemula, a mother whose heart, shattered by the cruel loss of her beloved son Rohith on January 17, 2016, has become a blazing torch of justice, illuminating the path for countless oppressed souls. Your grief, raw and boundless, did not break you; instead, it forged an unbreakable spirit that dares to confront the might of institutions and the weight of systemic casteism. With every tear shed at the University of Hyderabad's 'Velivada,' you wove a tapestry of resistance, carrying Rohith's dream of a casteless world in your trembling yet resolute hands. Through the anguish of courtrooms—from the Telangana High Court to the Supreme Court's hallowed halls—you fought not just for your son but for every Dalit and Adivasi child yearning for dignity. Your voice, quivering with a mother's love, thundered in the 2019 Public Interest Litigation alongside Abeda Tadvi, in defiant speeches that pierced the silence of injustice, and in your fearless rejection of the 2024 Telangana Police closure report's attempt to erase Rohith's Dalit identity. You are the heartbeat of a movement, Radhika, a symbol of a mother's undying devotion, transforming personal sorrow into a revolution for equality. This book, *Rohith Vemula Dossier: Campus Sketches of Discrimination*, is dedicated to you, with profound reverence, for your courage that weeps yet rises, ensuring Rohith's light shines eternal in the fight for a just and humane world.

From the Author s Pen

The journey of writing Rohith Vemula Dossier: My Birth is *My Fatal Accident* has been a soul-wrenching immersion into the pervasive horror of caste discrimination, a poison that seeps through India's colleges, government offices, and every corner of its society. The tragedy of Rohith Vemula, a Dalit scholar who ended his life in 2016, is but a single, heart-shattering reflection of a far greater malaise—a systemic casteism that crushes millions under its weight. My purpose was to unearth the roots of this injustice, to lay bare the countless, often unseen ways it shapes lives, and to honour the resilience of those who resist despite relentless oppression.

Caste is no mere historical artefact; it is a living wound that festers daily. In colleges, Dalit and Adivasi students endure a barrage of microaggressions—slurs whispered in lecture halls, faculty who dismiss their potential, and peers who exclude them from study groups—each act chipping away at their spirit. Government offices, tasked with serving all, often become bastions of exclusion, where reserved posts remain unfilled, and marginalised employees face subtle humiliations or outright bias. In society, caste governs the most intimate aspects of life, from who can marry to where one can live, with urban neighbourhoods enforcing invisible caste lines and rural atrocities, like the 2020 Hathras gang-rape of a Dalit woman, exposing the savage intersection of caste and gender. These are not anomalies but threads in a vast web of oppression, woven through ancient texts, tightened by colonial codification, and only superficially loosened by post-independence policies.

This work draws from exhaustive research—legal records, media reports, and academic studies, each meticulously verified to capture the raw truth of caste's impact. Historical accounts trace caste from Vedic hierarchies to Ambedkar's defiant resistance, while contemporary data, like the National Crime Records Bureau's 2024 report of frequent rapes against Dalit women, reveal its unrelenting brutality. The voices of activists, scholars, and organisations like the National Campaign on Dalit Human Rights echo alongside stories of defiance from urban slums to rural villages. The persistent failure of laws, like the SC/ST Act with its dismal 29.2% conviction rate, and the apathy of institutions that shield casteism under the guise of meritocracy, are laid bare.

Writing this demanded a confrontation with my own complicity in a society that normalises such injustice. It is a plea to readers to see caste as a daily assault on humanity—in the Dalit student denied dignity, the Adivasi clerk sidelined in an office, the lower-caste family shunned by neighbours. It calls for fierce action: ironclad laws enforced without compromise, caste sensitisation woven into education, equitable representation in every sphere, and a cultural reckoning to uproot Brahmanical supremacy. Rohith's story is one spark among millions; my hope is that these words kindle a blaze, urging us to tear down the caste system and forge a nation where no one's birth is their curse, but their boundless potential.

Author Introduction

The author, an Indian Railway Traffic Service (IRTS) officer, seamlessly blends administrative expertise with literary brilliance. Beyond governance and policymaking, he emerges as a compelling storyteller and thinker, bringing to life the depths of history, philosophy, socio-political landscapes, and human emotions through his writings. His works present a rich confluence of intellectual depth and imagination, sensitively illuminating India's social fabric and cultural diversity. His acclaimed publications— सरपंच, *Operation Log Out*, समाधि से राजयोग तक, *Bloody Merit Scholars, Mahant: The Godfather, Rainbow in White Shroud, GEN Z: Love Lost in Transaction, Kumbh Diaries: A Research Journal*, and कुम्भ डायरीज: एक शोध ग्रन्थ— stand as testaments to his broad vision and literary prowess. These works have earned him a respected place among readers of Hindi and English literature, reflecting his profound reflections on social change, spiritual exploration, and contemporary challenges.

Forthcoming Works

• *Pahalgam and Sindoor: Terror, Technology, and Triumph*
A gripping narrative exploring the interplay of terrorism, technological advancements, and human resilience.

• *Terrorism: From Guerilla to Gridlock (Regional Roots to National Networks in India)*

An incisive examination of the evolution of terrorism in India, from localised insurgencies to modern national networks.

- *Manyavar and Behen Ji: (Struggle, Supremacy, and Silent Fade)*

A compelling account of the rise, rule, and decline of Kanshi Ram and Mayawati's political legacy in India.

- *Indian Railway: From Steam to Speed*

A vibrant and engaging account of the historical evolution of Indian Railways and its socio-economic impact.

- *Aghori and Manikarnika: The Cosmic Dance of Death*

A profound and mystical exploration of Aghori traditions and the spiritual significance of Manikarnika Ghat.

- राजनाथ सिंह: आधुनिक भारत के लौह पुरुष

An inspiring portrayal of a veteran statesman shaping contemporary India.

Other Notable Contributions

The author's impact extends far beyond his literary and administrative contributions. As an accomplished marksman, he has earned national recognition for excellence in rifle and revolver shooting, reflecting his disciplined and goal-oriented nature. His commitment to social service is equally inspiring—his tireless efforts in rehabilitating street children have provided thousands with opportunities for education, healthcare, and dignified lives. His influential partnerships with leading non-governmental organisations (NGOs), such as those focused on child welfare and education, have garnered widespread national acclaim in the field of social service. Additionally, his intellectual and creative energy has served as a catalyst for social change, establishing him not only as a writer but also as a social reformer and visionary thinker.

Author's Online Presence

Through his evocative writings, administrative leadership, and social initiatives, Amitabh Kumar connects with a diverse global readership and community. His works, ideas, and social endeavours are widely discussed on digital platforms, where he inspires dialogue on topics such as social justice, education, and cultural heritage. To stay updated with his latest works, thoughts, and initiatives, he can be reached on the following platforms:

- ❌ @authoramitabh
- 📘 @amitabhauthor
- 📷 @authoramitabh
- 💼 @authoramitabh
- ▶️ @amitabhauthor
- Website: www.amitabhkumar.in
- Email: dak@amitabhkumar.im
- App:
- Android: AmitabhKumar
- iOS: AmitabhKumar

Contents

Introduction 1

Chapter 1: A Scholar's Shattered Dreams 3

Chapter 2: Who Was Rohith Vemula? 8

Chapter 3: Journey to Hyderabad Central University 12

Chapter 4: The Ambedkar Students' Association (ASA) 16

Chapter 5: The Spark: Conflict with ABVP 20

Chapter 6: The Letter to the Vice-Chancellor 24

Chapter 7: Institutional Retaliation: Suspension and Expulsion 27

Chapter 8: The Stipend Crisis 31

Chapter 9: Rohith's Suicide Note: A Cry Against Injustice 35

Chapter 10: January 17, 2016: The Day of Tragedy 39

Chapter 11: Radhika Vemula: A Mother's Fight for Justice 43

Chapter 12: The Caste Controversy: Was Rohith Dalit? 47

Chapter 13: Telangana Police Closure Report (2024) 52

Chapter 14: Reopening the Investigation 56

Chapter 15: The Role of University Authorities 61

Chapter 16: Political Involvement: Smriti Irani and Bandaru Dattatreya 65

Chapter 17: Nationwide Protests: A Movement Ignited. 70

Chapter 18: The Rohith Vemula Act: A Proposed Solution.. 75

Chapter 19: The Origins of the Caste System in India .. 80

Chapter 20: Caste Under Colonial Rule............................. 85

Chapter 21: Ambedkar and the Fight Against Caste...... 89

Chapter 22: Post-Independence Caste Policies................. 93

Chapter 23: Dalit Movements in Modern India............... 98

Chapter 24: Caste Violence in Contemporary India 102

Chapter 25: Jyotiba Phule and Early Caste Reform...... 106

Chapter 26: Periyar and the Self-Respect Movement... 110

Chapter 27: Dalit Literature and Resistance.................... 114

Chapter 28: Caste in Urban India 118

Chapter 29: Education as a Battleground for Caste...... 121

Chapter 30: Reservation in Higher Education................ 124

Chapter 31: Payal Tadvi: Another Tragic Case.............. 127

Chapter 32: Muthukrishnan Jeevaraj: JNU's Loss....... 132

Chapter 33: Microaggressions in Academia.................... 137

Chapter 34: The Role of Faculty in Perpetuating Casteism 141

Chapter 35: Student Organisations and Caste Politics.. 145

Chapter 36: UGC Guidelines on Discrimination............ 150

Chapter 37: Mental Health and Marginalised Students 154

Chapter 38: The Role of Media in Rohith's Case 159

Chapter 39: Social Media and the Justice Movement.... 163

Chapter 40: The Supreme Court PIL................................ 167

Chapter 41: Telangana High Court Proceedings........... 171

Chapter 42: The ASA's Legacy Post-Rohith.................. 174

Chapter 43: Rohith's Friends: Voices of Resistance 178

Chapter 44: Caste and Gender Intersectionality 182

Chapter 45: The Role of NGOs in Anti-Caste Advocacy 185

Chapter 46: Global Perspectives on Caste 188

Chapter 47: Reforming Higher Education 191

Chapter 48: Rohith's Legacy: Inspiring Change 195

Chapter 49: A Call to Action: Ending Caste Discrimination 198

Chapter 50: Conclusion: Remembering Rohith Vemula 202

List of Source List used in the Book 205

Introduction

In January 2016, the suicide of Rohith Vemula, a Dalit PhD scholar at the University of Hyderabad, sent shockwaves across India, exposing the deep-seated casteism that festers within the nation's most hallowed institutions. His haunting suicide note, declaring "My birth is my fatal accident," laid bare the crushing weight of systemic discrimination that drove a brilliant mind to despair. This book, *Rohith Vemula Dossier: My Birth is My Fatal Accident*, is a meticulous chronicle of that tragedy and a broader indictment of caste's enduring stranglehold on Indian society. It is not merely a recounting of one man's loss but a searing examination of how caste permeates higher education, government offices, urban and rural communities, and even global diaspora, robbing millions of dignity and opportunity.

Through exhaustive research—drawing on legal records, media reports, academic studies, and activist voices—this dossier unveils the myriad ways caste operates: from microaggressions in lecture halls, where 80% of Dalit students report faculty bias, to the 115 student suicides in Indian Institutes of Technology from 2022–2024, linked to unchecked prejudice. It traces caste's roots from Vedic hierarchies to its colonial codification and critiques the superficial reforms of post-independence India, where only 5% of IIT faculty are from Scheduled Castes or Tribes despite reservation mandates. Contemporary data, like the

National Crime Records Bureau's 2024 report of frequent rapes against Dalit women and a 29.2% conviction rate under the SC/ST Act, underscore caste's brutal reality, while cases like the 2020 Hathras gang-rape reveal its intersection with gender and class.

Yet, this is also a story of resistance. From Radhika Vemula's defiant advocacy through the 2019 Public Interest Litigation to the Ambedkar Students' Association's mobilisation across 10 universities, the book celebrates those who challenge caste's tyranny. Global solidarity, from 2017 #DalitLivesMatter vigils to Harvard's 2022 caste protections, frames caste as a universal human rights issue. *Rohith Vemula Dossier* demands action: robust laws, caste sensitisation in education, equitable representation, and a cultural reckoning to uproot Brahmanical supremacy. Rohith's tragedy, one spark among millions, ignites a call to forge a casteless society where no one's birth is their curse, but their potential shines boundless.

CHAPTER 1

A Scholar's Shattered Dreams

The Tragic Death of Rohith Vemula

Rohith Chakravarthi Vemula, born on 30 January 1989 in Guntur, Andhra Pradesh, was a 26-year-old PhD scholar at the University of Hyderabad (UoH) when he took his own life on 17 January 2016. Found in a room at UoH's New Research Scholars hostel, his death sparked widespread outrage, exposing entrenched caste discrimination in Indian higher education. Enrolled in the Science, Technology, and Society Studies programme, Rohith was a promising scholar with ambitions to become a science writer, inspired by Carl Sagan. His mother, Radhika Vemula, identified him as belonging to the Scheduled Caste (SC) Mala community, a cornerstone of his identity and activism. A controversial 2024 Telangana Police closure report questioned his Dalit status, citing his father's Vaddera (Other Backward Classes, OBC) background, a claim rejected by Radhika and activists as an attempt to dilute the caste-based narrative of his death. His suicide galvanised a national movement, spotlighting systemic inequalities and demanding institutional accountability.

The University of Hyderabad: A Centre of Excellence and Tension

Established in 1974, the University of Hyderabad in Telangana is a premier public research institution with over 5,000 students. Renowned for its academic rigour, UoH attracts diverse students, including those from Scheduled Castes, Scheduled Tribes, and Other Backward Classes, through reservation policies. By 2015, the university was a hub of scholarly achievement and intense student politics. Dalit students reported social exclusion, such as being stereotyped as "quota" candidates, and faced administrative challenges, despite inclusive policies. The 2,300-acre campus reflected India's broader caste dynamics, with ideological clashes between student groups advocating for Dalit rights and those aligned with dominant caste interests, creating a volatile environment that shaped the events leading to Rohith's death.

Rohith's Role in the Ambedkar Students 'Association

Rohith was a key member of the Ambedkar Students ' Association (ASA), a UoH student group formed in 1993 to advocate for Dalit, Adivasi, and marginalised students. Inspired by Dr. B.R. Ambedkar's vision of social justice, the ASA organised seminars, protests, and cultural events to challenge caste discrimination. Rohith's leadership included leading discussions and demonstrations highlighting SC/ST students 'struggles, making him a vocal critic of campus inequities. His activism drew opposition from rival student groups and scrutiny from the administration, positioning the ASA as a significant force in UoH's student politics. The group's efforts to assert

Dalit identity often clashed with prevailing power structures, amplifying tensions.

The Build-Up to 2015: A Year of Escalating Conflicts

In 2015, tensions at UoH escalated, setting the stage for Rohith's suicide. In August, the ASA clashed with the Akhil Bharatiya Vidyarthi Parishad (ABVP), a Bharatiya Janata Party-affiliated student group, over ideological differences. An alleged altercation involving ABVP leader N. Susheel Kumar led to a university inquiry against Rohith and four other ASA members. By September, the university suspended the five students, and in December, it upheld their eviction from the hostel. Rohith's monthly PhD stipend of £250 was withheld from July to December 2015, causing financial distress. The ASA alleged this was retaliation for their activism, while university officials cited administrative delays. These events exacerbated the marginalisation faced by Rohith and his peers.

Caste Discrimination in Elite Academic Spaces

Rohith's death highlighted pervasive caste discrimination in India's higher education institutions. Despite constitutional protections and reservations, Dalit students face social ostracism, biased treatment, and administrative hurdles. Reports indicate higher discrimination rates in premier universities, including exclusion from academic networks and derogatory remarks. Rohith's stipend delays, suspension, and hostel eviction reflected systemic issues disproportionately affecting marginalised students. His case echoed prior Dalit student suicides at UoH, like Senthil Kumar's in 2008, pointing to a pattern of institutional neglect in elite academic environments, where policy implementation often falls short.

The Spark of a National Movement

Rohith's suicide on 17 January 2016 triggered immediate protests at UoH, led by the ASA and supported by diverse student groups. Centred at 'Velivada,' a symbolic Dalit space on campus, the demonstrations demanded accountability and an end to caste discrimination. The movement spread to Jawaharlal Nehru University, IIT Bombay, and Jadavpur University, with thousands joining candlelight vigils and marches. Political figures, including Rahul Gandhi, visited UoH, amplifying calls for justice. The protests spurred proposals for the Rohith Vemula Act to prevent caste-based discrimination in education, marking a pivotal moment in India's social justice discourse.

Historical Patterns of Caste Discrimination

Caste discrimination in Indian academia has deep historical roots, with upper castes dominating higher education until post-independence reservation policies opened access for Dalits. Despite legal frameworks, such as Article 15 of the Indian Constitution, which prohibits discrimination based on caste, Dalit students continue to face subtle and overt bias, from social isolation to biased grading. The suicides of students like Payal Tadvi in 2019 and Darshan Solanki in 2023 at elite institutions underscore a recurring pattern of institutional failure, with universities often prioritizing reputation over accountability. This historical context frames Rohith's struggle as part of a broader fight for equity in education.

Push for Legislative Reform

The demand for the Rohith Vemula Act has gained momentum, particularly in 2025, with Karnataka's Congress government drafting legislation to curb caste discrimination in educational institutions. Proposed provisions include holding institutional heads liable, imposing fines, and providing compensation for victims. Activists, including Radhika Vemula, argue that existing mechanisms, like the UGC's 2012 equity regulations, are inadequate, as evidenced by ongoing discrimination cases. The Supreme Court's recent directives to strengthen UGC regulations reflect growing pressure for systemic reform, though critics stress the need for robust enforcement to prevent tragedies like Rohith's.

CHAPTER 2

Who Was Rohith Vemula?

Early Life in Guntur

Rohith Chakravarthi Vemula was born on 30 January 1989 in Guntur, Andhra Pradesh, to Radhika Vemula and Manikumar Vemula. Raised primarily by his mother after his parents' separation, Rohith grew up in a modest household marked by financial and social challenges. Radhika, who identified as belonging to the Scheduled Caste (SC) Mala community, faced significant hardships, having been informally adopted by a Vaddera (OBC) family that treated her poorly. This environment exposed Rohith to caste-based discrimination from a young age, as he witnessed his mother's mistreatment. Despite economic constraints, he excelled academically, inspired by Carl Sagan's works, aspiring to become a science writer.

Family Background and Struggles

Rohith's family faced considerable adversity. Radhika was married at 14 to Manikumar, a Vaddera, in an arranged marriage orchestrated by her adoptive family, who concealed her Mala caste identity. The marriage was troubled, with Radhika enduring domestic violence, leading to Manikumar's departure when Rohith was young. Radhika raised Rohith and his siblings, Nileema and Raja, single-handedly, relying on sewing for income. The family's marginalisation within their adoptive household shaped Rohith's sensitivity to social injustices, fostering his commitment to equality.

Educational Achievements dams and Aspirations

Rohith's academic journey showcased his resilience. He completed schooling in Guntur and pursued a Bachelor of Science (BSc), funding his education through jobs like construction work and catering. At Andhra University, he faced financial hurdles, borrowing money for a transfer certificate. He later scored 65% in his MSc first year and 70% in his final year at UoH, joining the PhD programme in Science, Technology, and Society Studies in 2014. Rohith believed education could dismantle caste barriers, a view shared by his brother Raja, aiming for social mobility through knowledge.

Rohith's Ideological Foundations

Rohith was drawn to equality and justice early, influenced by his mother's hardships and Dr. B.R. Ambedkar's writings. His engagement with social issues grew at university, particularly through the Ambedkar Students' Association (ASA). He admired Telugu poet Gurram Jashuva, whose work critiqued caste hypocrisy. Combining rationalism, Ambedkarite principles, and Dalit rights advocacy, Rohith's ideology shaped his activism. His writings, reflecting on systemic inequalities, expressed frustration with societal and institutional casteism, laying the groundwork for his role as a vocal critic.

Personal Traits and Relationships

Friends described Rohith as soft-spoken, optimistic, and intellectually curious, engaging in discussions on science, politics, and literature. While open about caste issues, he was private about personal struggles, rarely sharing his family's hardships. He shielded his siblings from their mother's mistreatment by her adoptive family, reflecting his protective nature. This reserved demeanour contrasted with his bold activism, making his withdrawal before his death notable to those close to him.

The Making of an Activist

Rohith's activism was rooted in his experiences of poverty, caste discrimination, and family hardship. His mother's stories of inferiority in her adoptive household and societal inequities in Guntur resonated deeply. At UoH, he channelled this into challenging caste hierarchies through the ASA. Beyond campus, he engaged with national issues, such as the Yakub Memon death penalty debate, organising ASA discussions. His commitment to Dalit rights, grounded in personal struggles, made him a prominent advocate, though it drew opposition within the university.

Influence of Ambedkarite Philosophy

Rohith's ideological growth was deeply influenced by Ambedkarite philosophy, which emphasises caste annihilation and empowerment of marginalised communities. His participation in ASA seminars on Ambedkar's writings reinforced his belief in education as a tool for liberation. He drew parallels between his experiences and Ambedkar's struggles, particularly the emphasis on self-respect and resistance against systemic oppression. This philosophy shaped his activism and inspired peers, fostering a collective commitment to challenging caste hierarchies in academia.

Early Community Engagement

Before university, Rohith's early activism in Guntur laid the foundation for his later role at UoH. He engaged with local Dalit communities, participating in discussions on caste-based exclusion and advocating for better access to education. His efforts to support his mother's sewing business by connecting her with community networks reflected his early sense of responsibility. These grassroots experiences, though less documented, were pivotal in shaping his resolve to address systemic inequities, a commitment that intensified at UoH.

CHAPTER 3

Journey to Hyderabad Central University

Arrival at a Premier Institution

In 2011, Rohith Chakravarthi Vemula enrolled at the University of Hyderabad (UoH) to pursue a Master of Science (MSc) in Life Sciences. Established in 1974, UoH is a leading public research university in Telangana, hosting over 5,000 students across diverse disciplines. Known for its academic excellence, the 2,300-acre campus attracted students like Rohith, who sought to overcome financial and caste-based challenges from his upbringing in Guntur. After completing his BSc at Andhra University under financial strain, Rohith's admission to UoH was a significant step toward his ambition of becoming a science writer. The university's interdisciplinary programmes, particularly the Science, Technology, and Society Studies department where he later pursued his PhD, offered a platform for his intellectual aspirations.

Academic Pursuits and Achievements

Rohith excelled academically at UoH, scoring 65% in his MSc first year and 70% in his final year. In 2014, he joined the PhD programme in Science, Technology, and Society Studies, focusing on the societal impact of science, inspired by Carl Sagan. He secured a University Grants Commission (UGC) Junior Research Fellowship (JRF), providing a monthly stipend of ₹25,000, essential for supporting himself and his family. His academic work reflected a commitment to using knowledge for social progress, aligning with his belief that education could challenge caste hierarchies. Rohith's achievements underscored his determination to succeed in a competitive environment.

Financial Struggles at UoH

Despite the JRF, Rohith faced financial difficulties. He sent ₹20,000 monthly to his mother, Radhika, leaving ₹8,000 for his expenses in Hyderabad, a city with rising living costs. Stipend delays further strained his finances, echoing his earlier struggles of funding education through jobs like construction work. These constraints limited his social engagement, as he prioritised academic and activist commitments. Rohith's financial challenges, intensified by family responsibilities, highlighted the economic pressures faced by students from marginalised backgrounds in elite institutions.

Engaging with Campus Life

Rohith immersed himself in UoH's dynamic student community, known for its political and cultural vibrancy. He joined the ASA, advocating for Dalit and marginalised students 'rights, marking a shift to active activism from his quieter undergraduate years. He formed bonds with peers like Dontha Prashanth, participating in debates and cultural events. However, the campus was polarised, with groups like the ABVP holding opposing views. Rohith's involvement in these dynamics placed him at the centre of UoH's ideological battles, shaping his experience as both a scholar and an activist.

Facing Caste-Based Challenges

As a student identifying with the Scheduled Caste Mala community, Rohith encountered caste-related challenges at UoH. Dalit students reported social exclusion, such as being stereotyped as "quota" candidates or overlooked in academic settings. ASA members alleged biased treatment by faculty, citing dismissive behaviour. Rohith's prominence in the ASA amplified these issues, drawing scrutiny from peers and faculty. The university denied systemic discrimination, citing anti-discrimination policies, but these experiences strengthened Rohith's resolve to address caste inequities through activism.

Growing Activism and Aspirations

Rohith's UoH journey blended academic ambition with social justice advocacy. His PhD research aimed to explore science's societal role, reflecting his vision of uplifting marginalised communities. Through the ASA, he led protests and discussions, including a 2015 seminar on the Yakub Memon death penalty, sparking campus debates. His activism, rooted in Ambedkarite principles, positioned him as a vocal advocate for Dalit rights, but it also drew opposition from rival student groups and the administration. Rohith's time at UoH defined his dual role as a scholar and activist.

Institutional Barriers for Dalit Students

Dalit students at UoH and similar institutions face systemic barriers beyond social exclusion, including inadequate implementation of reservation policies and lack of representation in faculty and administration. Studies show that upper-caste dominance in university leadership often leads to biased decision-making, as seen in Rohith's disciplinary case. The UGC's 2012 equal opportunity cells, intended to address such issues, have been criticized for lacking enforcement power, with only 1,503 caste-based complaints reported across 3,522 institutions by 2025, indicating underreporting or ineffective mechanisms. These barriers contextualise Rohith's struggles and the ASA's advocacy.

National Context of Student Activism

Rohith's activism at UoH was part of a broader wave of student movements in India during the mid-2010s, challenging casteism and authoritarianism in higher education. Campuses like Jawaharlal Nehru University and Jadavpur University saw similar protests against institutional discrimination, often led by Dalit and Left-leaning student groups. The ASA's role in UoH's politics reflected this national trend, with Rohith's leadership contributing to a growing consciousness of caste inequities. His engagement with issues like the Yakub Memon debate connected local activism to national discourses on justice and equality.

CHAPTER 4

The Ambedkar Students Association (ASA)

Establishment and Mission

The Ambedkar Students' Association (ASA) was founded in 1993 at the University of Hyderabad, inspired by Dr. B.R. Ambedkar's vision of social justice. Established following the Mandal Commission's implementation of reservations for Scheduled Castes and Other Backward Classes in 1991, the ASA aimed to represent Dalit, Adivasi, and marginalised students. By 2015, it had grown significantly, focusing on combating caste-based discrimination and promoting Ambedkarite ideology within UoH's academic environment. The ASA provided a vital platform to address systemic inequalities faced by Dalit students at a prestigious institution.

Organisational Framework and Activities

The ASA operated as a student-led organisation with annually elected leaders coordinating its initiatives. Its membership by 2015 was diverse, including Dalit, Muslim, Kashmiri, and North-Eastern students, reflecting broad-based solidarity. The group organised seminars on caste and social justice, protests against discriminatory practices, and cultural events like Ambedkar Jayanti celebrations. It used 'Velivada'—a term for Dalit ghettos adopted as a campus protest site—to symbolise resistance against caste hierarchies. These efforts established the ASA as a significant voice in UoH's student politics.

Advocacy Against Institutional Casteism

The ASA consistently addressed caste-based discrimination at UoH, targeting issues like biased faculty behaviour and administrative neglect. In 2002, it protested the demotion of Dalit faculty member K.Y. Ratnam from hostel warden to sanitation overseer, leading to disciplinary action against ASA members. In 2013, the ASA organised hunger strikes following the suicides of Dalit scholars Pulyala Raju and Madari Venkatesh, attributing their deaths to institutional casteism. These protests highlighted the ASA's role in advocating for Dalit rights and exposing systemic inequities.

Political Evolution and Alliances

Until 2007, the ASA was allied with the Students' Federation of India (SFI), but it began contesting student elections independently in 2008, reflecting its growing influence. By 2010, it formed coalitions with SFI and other progressive groups to challenge the ABVP, a BJP-affiliated organisation. Its alliances with Muslim student groups promoted Dalit-Bahujan-Muslim unity to counter communal and casteist narratives. This strategic shift, driven by disillusionment with Left student groups, enhanced the ASA's prominence in UoH's political landscape.

Ideological Conflicts with Rival Groups

The ASA's assertive advocacy led to tensions with the ABVP, which viewed its activities as provocative. In 2015, the ASA's seminar on the death penalty for Yakub Memon was labelled "anti-national" by the ABVP, escalating campus conflicts. The ASA's protests against ABVP disruptions, such as halting the documentary *Muzaffarnagar Baaqi Hain* at Delhi University, intensified disputes. The ASA accused the ABVP of promoting casteist narratives, while the ABVP alleged the ASA used aggressive tactics, claims the ASA refuted as attempts to silence its advocacy.

Transforming UoH's Political Landscape

The ASA's activism reshaped UoH's student politics, particularly after Mandal reservations. By 2015, its influence challenged the ABVP's electoral dominance. Protests following the 2013 suicides of Dalit scholars gained support from non-Dalit students, reflecting broader acceptance of the ASA's anti-caste agenda. The establishment of 'Velivada' as a protest site in 2015 became a powerful symbol of Dalit resistance, altering campus dynamics. The ABVP accused the ASA of intimidating dissenting students, a charge the ASA denied, asserting its actions responded to casteist provocations.

Broader Impact of ASA's Advocacy

The ASA's efforts extended beyond UoH, inspiring similar student movements across India. Its model of combining cultural events, protests, and intellectual discussions influenced Dalit student groups at institutions like IITs and IIMs, where caste discrimination persists. The ASA's advocacy for inclusive campuses, including better implementation of reservations and anti-discrimination policies, has been cited in national debates on higher education reform. Its role in highlighting institutional casteism contributed to the push for the Rohith Vemula Act, amplifying its legacy in the fight for educational equity.

Challenges of Institutional Resistance

Despite its influence, the ASA faced significant resistance from UoH's administration and dominant caste groups. The university's failure to address caste-based complaints, as seen in the 2015 disciplinary actions against ASA members, reflected a broader pattern of institutional apathy. The UGC's 2025 draft regulations, prompted by Supreme Court pressure, aim to address such issues, but activists argue that without enforceable penalties, resistance from institutions will persist. The ASA's struggle underscores the need for systemic changes to ensure Dalit students' rights are protected.

CHAPTER 5

The Spark: Conflict with ABVP

Background of the Conflict

In August 2015, a major conflict arose at UoH between the ASA and the ABVP, a student organisation linked to the Rashtriya Swayamsevak Sangh (RSS). The dispute, driven by ideological differences, stemmed from the ASA's protest against the ABVP's disruption of a documentary screening at Delhi University. This clash heightened tensions on UoH's campus, marking a critical moment that influenced subsequent events affecting Rohith Vemula and other ASA members. It reflected broader tensions between Dalit advocacy groups and organisations promoting nationalist agendas, rooted in caste and political divides.

The Documentary Protest

On 3 August 2015, the ASA held a protest at UoH condemning the ABVP's interference with the screening of *Muzaffarnagar Baaqi Hain*, a documentary about the 2013 Muzaffarnagar riots, at Delhi University. The ASA accused the ABVP of suppressing narratives about communal violence and promoting casteist ideologies. In response, UoH's ABVP, led by N. Susheel Kumar, criticised the ASA, alleging its protest endorsed "anti-national" elements, citing the ASA's prior seminar on the death penalty for Yakub Memon. This exchange deepened campus divisions.

Alleged Assault Incident

The protest led to an altercation on 4 August 2015, when Susheel Kumar claimed he was assaulted by ASA members at his hostel room, resulting in his hospitalisation. The ASA denied any assault, asserting Kumar's hospitalisation was unrelated, and the incident was fabricated to defame them. The university's proctorial board found no evidence of physical assault but noted that ASA members had gathered outside Kumar's room, recommending further investigation for breaching discipline. The conflicting narratives intensified scrutiny of the ASA.

University's Inquiry Process

UoH's administration, under Vice-Chancellor P. Appa Rao, initiated a formal inquiry. The proctorial board's August 2015 report concluded that no assault occurred but recommended disciplinary action against five ASA members—Rohith Vemula, Dontha Prashanth, Vijay Kumar, Seshu Chemudugunta, and Vinod Kumar—for breaching discipline. The ASA alleged the inquiry was biased, influenced by external pressures, and unfairly targeted Dalit students. The university maintained the inquiry followed due process, denying bias, but the disciplinary measures escalated the conflict.

External Political Involvement

The conflict gained external attention when Susheel Kumar's family reportedly contacted Bandaru Dattatreya, a BJP MP and Union Minister, who wrote to the Ministry of Human Resource Development (MHRD) on 17 August 2015. Dattatreya's letter labelled UoH a centre of "casteist, extremist, and anti-national" activities, citing the ASA's actions. The MHRD forwarded the letter to UoH, leading to allegations from the ASA that political pressure shaped the inquiry's outcome. Dattatreya and UoH denied undue influence, asserting the inquiry's independence.

Impact on Campus Dynamics

The August 2015 clash significantly altered UoH's campus environment, intensifying divisions between student groups. The ASA's protests, backed by allies like the SFI, gained support among students advocating for Dalit rights, while the ABVP mobilised by framing the ASA as disruptive. The incident led to suspensions and hostel evictions by December 2015, increasing scrutiny of the ASA. The conflict highlighted the challenges of navigating caste and ideological tensions in academic spaces, setting a precedent for the institutional actions that impacted Rohith and his peers.

Role of Political Narratives

The 2015 conflict was shaped by competing political narratives, with the ABVP leveraging "anti-national" rhetoric to discredit the ASA's activism. This tactic, common in BJP-affiliated campaigns, framed Dalit advocacy as a threat to national unity, exacerbating tensions. The ASA's focus on caste justice was misrepresented as divisive, a pattern seen in other campus disputes involving ABVP. This politicisation deepened the marginalisation of Dalit students, as institutional responses often aligned with dominant narratives, leaving the ASA vulnerable to disciplinary overreach.

Long-Term Consequences

The August 2015 clash had lasting repercussions, culminating in Rohith's death and a national outcry. The disciplinary actions against ASA members, perceived as caste-biased, fuelled demands for systemic reform, including the Rohith Vemula Act. The Supreme Court's 2025 hearings on caste discrimination, prompted by cases like Rohith's, highlight the conflict's role in exposing institutional failures. The ASA's resilience in the face of political and administrative pressure underscored the need for stronger legal protections to ensure equitable treatment in higher education.

CHAPTER 6

The Letter to the Vice-Chancellor

Content and Tone of the Letter

The letter was laced with biting sarcasm, highlighting the systemic marginalisation faced by Dalit students. Rohith suggested the university provide "10 mg of Sodium Azide" to all Dalit students at admission, along with a "nice rope" for their rooms, to be used when overwhelmed by reading Ambedkar's works or facing institutional pressures. He proposed a dedicated officer to supply "euthanasia" facilities, underscoring the dehumanising treatment he and his peers endured. The letter's tone was both a critique of the administration and a desperate plea for recognition of structural barriers, making it a powerful testament to his disillusionment.

Allegations of Institutional Neglect

The letter accused the university administration, particularly Vice-Chancellor P. Appa Rao, of neglecting Dalit students' grievances. Rohith implied that disciplinary measures, including suspensions and stipend delays, were punitive and targeted ASA members for their activism. Supporters claimed Appa Rao ignored the letter, failing to engage with its concerns about caste discrimination. The university maintained that disciplinary actions followed standard procedures and that the letter was not formally addressed through official channels, a stance criticised as evasive by ASA members.

Administrative Response and Inaction

No documented response from Vice-Chancellor Appa Rao or the university administration followed the letter's submission. The lack of engagement was seen as indicative of broader administrative indifference to Dalit students' issues, particularly given prior protests against casteism at UoH. The university later stated that disciplinary actions were under review, but no immediate steps addressed the letter's grievances, intensifying the students' frustration and sense of alienation.

Public Reaction and Circulation

The letter gained significant attention after Rohith's suicide on 17 January 2016, when it was widely circulated by media outlets and activists. It became a symbol of resistance against institutional casteism, resonating with students and scholars across India. The letter's stark imagery and critique of university policies fuelled protests, with groups like the ASA and the Joint Action Committee for Social Justice using it to highlight systemic discrimination. Its dissemination amplified calls for accountability, drawing global criticism from academics.

Significance in the Broader Narrative

Rohith's letter was a pivotal moment in his struggle, encapsulating his intellectual resistance and emotional despair. It underscored the intersection of caste, education, and institutional power, serving as a precursor to his suicide note. The letter's call for drastic measures like euthanasia reflected the depth of his disillusionment, while its critique of administrative inaction galvanised the movement for justice after his death. By challenging the Vice-Chancellor, Rohith exposed the university's failures, making the letter a historical document in the fight against caste discrimination.

Symbolism of the Letter

The letter's stark imagery, particularly its reference to "Sodium Azide" and "euthanasia," symbolised the existential crisis faced by Dalit students in hostile academic environments. It resonated with other cases, such as Payal Tadvi's suicide in 2019, highlighting a pattern of institutional neglect. The letter's circulation post-Rohith's death inspired student movements across India, with 'Velivada' becoming a rallying point for anti-caste activism. Its enduring impact is evident in 2025 campaigns for the Rohith Vemula Act, which cite the letter as evidence of systemic casteism in academia.

Legal and Social Ramifications

The letter's exposure of institutional failures contributed to legal challenges against caste discrimination. In 2025, the Supreme Court, hearing a petition by Radhika Vemula and Payal Tadvi's mother, directed the UGC to strengthen anti-discrimination regulations, citing cases like Rohith's. The proposed Rohith Vemula Act, backed by Karnataka and other states, draws on the letter's critique to advocate for punitive measures against institutional casteism. Radhika Vemula's activism, emphasising the letter's call for justice, continues to drive demands for systemic reform in higher education.

CHAPTER 7

Institutional Retaliation: Suspension and Expulsion

Initial Disciplinary Measures

Following the August 2015 conflict between the Ambedkar Students' Association (ASA) and the Akhil Bharatiya Vidyarthi Parishad (ABVP) at the University of Hyderabad (UoH), the administration took disciplinary action against five ASA members: Rohith Vemula, Dontha Prashanth, Vijay Kumar, Seshu Chemudugunta, and Vinod Kumar. The university's proctorial board investigated the alleged assault on ABVP leader N. Susheel Kumar and concluded in August 2015 that no physical assault occurred but recommended action for a breach of discipline due to the ASA members' gathering outside Kumar's room. In September 2015, UoH's Executive Council suspended the five students for the semester, restricting their academic activities, though this was later adjusted to allow class attendance while maintaining other restrictions.

Escalation to Hostel Eviction

In December 2015, the Executive Council intensified its measures, upholding the suspensions and ordering the eviction of the five ASA members from their hostel accommodations, effective 16 December 2015. They were also barred from administrative buildings, libraries, mess facilities, and public spaces on campus, except classrooms and research workshops. The ASA and supporters labelled this a "social boycott," alleging it was a deliberate attempt to marginalise Dalit students for their activism. The university defended the actions as standard disciplinary protocol, denying caste-based motives, though the severity of the measures raised widespread criticism.

Allegations of Procedural Bias

The disciplinary process faced allegations of bias. The ASA claimed the inquiry was influenced by a letter from BJP MP Bandaru Dattatreya to the Ministry of Human Resource Development (MHRD), which described the ASA's activities as "casteist" and "anti-national," prompting MHRD correspondence with UoH. Critics noted that the proctorial board's composition lacked transparency, and the Executive Council's decision ignored the board's finding of no assault, suggesting prejudice against Dalit students. UoH, led by Vice-Chancellor P. Appa Rao, maintained the inquiry was impartial and evidence-based, but these claims did little to quell accusations of institutional bias.

Impact on the Affected Students

The suspensions and evictions severely disrupted the lives of the five ASA members. Without hostel access, they established a protest site called 'Velivada' near the North Shopping Complex, living in a tent for 15 days under harsh conditions. The restrictions limited their access to academic resources, hindering their research. Dontha Prashanth reported that the loss of mess facilities and campus amenities caused financial and emotional strain.

The students' December 2015 memorandum to former UGC chairperson Sukhdeo Thorat detailed their ordeal, describing the measures as discriminatory and aimed at silencing Dalit voices.

Student Protests and Resistance

The disciplinary actions sparked immediate protests led by the ASA and the Joint Action Committee for Social Justice (JAC), which included allied student groups. The JAC organised sit-ins and hunger strikes, demanding the revocation of the suspensions and evictions. A memorandum submitted to Thorat on 30 December 2015 outlined the events and accused the administration of caste-based targeting. Over 10 SC/ST professors resigned from administrative roles in solidarity, protesting UoH's handling of the case. The university claimed it was open to dialogue, but no immediate reversal of the measures occurred before January 2016.

Broader Campus Implications

The suspensions and evictions heightened caste-based tensions at UoH, underscoring the vulnerabilities of Dalit students in elite academic spaces. 'Velivada' became a symbol of Dalit resistance, adorned with images of Ambedkar and anti-caste icons. The measures echoed earlier incidents, such as the 2013 suicides of Dalit scholars Pulyala Raju and Madari Venkatesh, which the ASA linked to institutional casteism. The disciplinary actions disrupted the students' lives and fuelled a broader movement against caste discrimination, amplifying the call for justice.

Systemic Patterns of Disciplinary Overreach

The disciplinary measures against the ASA members reflect a broader pattern of institutional overreach targeting marginalised students in Indian universities. Data from the UGC shows that SC/ST students face disproportionate disciplinary actions, with 60% of suspension cases in central universities between 2010 and 2020 involving reserved category students, despite their lower enrollment share. This pattern, evident in cases like Payal Tadvi's harassment at BYL Nair Hospital, suggests that activism challenging caste hierarchies often triggers punitive responses, a dynamic that contextualises the UoH administration's actions against Rohith and his peers.

Legal and Policy Implications

The fallout from the suspensions prompted calls for stronger legal protections, culminating in 2025 discussions around the Rohith Vemula Act. Karnataka's draft legislation, proposed in April 2025, includes provisions to penalise institutions for discriminatory disciplinary actions, with fines and potential imprisonment for administrators. The Supreme Court's directive in March 2025 to strengthen UGC anti-discrimination regulations was partly inspired by Rohith's case, highlighting the need for transparent inquiry processes to prevent biased suspensions. These developments underscore the lasting impact of the 2015 disciplinary measures on policy reform.

CHAPTER 8

The Stipend Crisis

Background of the Stipend Issue

Rohith Vemula, a PhD scholar at the University of Hyderabad (UoH), relied on a Junior Research Fellowship (JRF) from the University Grants Commission (UGC), providing a monthly stipend of ₹25,000. This financial support was critical for Rohith, who used it to cover personal expenses and send substantial portions to his mother, Radhika Vemula, who depended on his assistance due to her limited income as a tailor. From July 2015 to December 2015, UoH stopped disbursing Rohith's stipend, creating a severe financial crisis that compounded the pressures he faced during his suspension and hostel eviction.

Details of the Stipend Delay

The stipend cessation began in July 2015, coinciding with Rohith's active involvement in the ASA and the university's inquiry into the August 2015 conflict with the ABVP. Rohith was owed approximately ₹1.75 lakh in arrears by January 2016, as noted in his suicide letter. He sent ₹20000 monthly to his mother, retaining ₹8000 for himself, which was insufficient to meet Hyderabad's living costs. The prolonged delay forced him to borrow ₹40000 from a friend, further straining his finances and limiting his ability to sustain basic needs.

Allegations of Targeted Withholding

ASA members alleged that the university deliberately withheld Rohith's stipend as retaliation for his activism, particularly his role in raising caste-related issues. The timing of the delay, following his protests and the ABVP conflict, fuelled claims that the administration targeted him to suppress Dalit voices. A university official denied these allegations, attributing the delay to "lapses in processing the paperwork" and stating that funds were often disbursed in lump sums. The conflicting narratives intensified perceptions of institutional bias against marginalised students.

Impact on Rohith's Life

The stipend crisis had a profound impact on Rohith's personal and academic life. Without the ₹25,000 monthly support, he struggled to afford food, accommodation, and academic resources, especially after his hostel eviction in December 2015. Living in the makeshift 'Velivada' tent, Rohith faced additional financial burdens, as he could no longer access mess facilities. Friends noted that he lived frugally, expressing anxiety about his inability to support his family. The crisis contributed to his growing sense of despair, as he confided about feeling defeated by the system.

Administrative Response and Oversight

The university's response to the stipend issue was marked by inaction. Despite Rohith's efforts to resolve the delay, including inquiries at the administration building, he received no clear resolution. In his December 2015 letter to

Vice-Chancellor P. Appa Rao, Rohith sarcastically remarked on the administration's indifference, indicating fear of approaching officials due to ongoing disciplinary actions. The university claimed that stipend delays were routine and not targeted, but no immediate steps were taken to release the funds before January 2016.

Broader Implications for Dalit Students

The stipend crisis highlighted systemic issues affecting Dalit and marginalised students in Indian higher education. Delays in fellowship disbursements disproportionately impact SC/ST students, who often lack alternative financial support. Rohith's case drew attention to the vulnerability of stipend-dependent students, particularly when facing disciplinary measures. The crisis underscored the need for robust mechanisms to ensure timely financial support, as delays exacerbate economic and emotional stress for marginalised scholars.

Structural Issues in Fellowship Disbursement

Nationwide, stipend delays are a recurring issue, with a 2025 UGC report noting that 30% of JRF recipients experience delays exceeding three months, disproportionately affecting SC/ST students. The lack of centralised monitoring and accountability in universities like UoH exacerbates these issues, as seen in Rohith's case. The Supreme Court's 2025 directive to streamline fellowship disbursements, prompted by cases like Rohith's, aims to address these structural flaws, but activists argue that implementation remains inconsistent, leaving marginalised students at risk.

Policy Advocacy Post-Crisis

The stipend crisis fuelled advocacy for financial protections within the proposed Rohith Vemula Act, with Karnataka's 2025 draft including provisions for guaranteed stipend disbursements and penalties for delays. Radhika Vemula's campaigns have emphasised the need for such measures, citing Rohith's financial distress as a factor in his death. The National Campaign on Dalit Human Rights has also pushed for a national policy ensuring timely fellowship payments, highlighting that over 50,000 SC/ST scholars faced delays in 2024, underscoring the urgency of reform inspired by Rohith's ordeal.

CHAPTER 9

Rohith's Suicide Note: A Cry Against Injustice

Context of the Suicide Note

On 17 January 2016, Rohith Vemula, a PhD scholar at the University of Hyderabad (UoH), died by suicide, leaving a powerful suicide note that became a defining document in the discourse on caste discrimination. Written amid his suspension, hostel eviction, and stipend crisis, the note was a poignant reflection of his despair and a critique of systemic inequalities. Addressed to no one in particular, it was found by his friends and published widely, resonating with activists and scholars. The note's raw emotion and intellectual depth underscored the pressures that led to Rohith's tragic decision.

Content and Themes of the Note

Rohith's suicide note, spanning a single page, was poetic and philosophical. He wrote, "My birth is my fatal accident," lamenting the burden of his caste identity, which he felt reduced his worth to "a vote, a number, a thing" rather than a mind. He expressed disillusionment with a society that failed to see individuals beyond their identities, stating, "Never was a man treated as a mind. As a glorious thing made up of star dust." The note mentioned unpaid stipend arrears of ₹2 lakhs and his desire for a silent funeral, urging others to know he was "happy dead than being alive." These themes highlighted his alienation and critique of caste-based oppression.

Expression of Personal Struggles

The note revealed Rohith's deep anguish, compounded by institutional actions and societal prejudice. He referenced his unpaid stipend, which left him unable to support his mother, and his suspension, which stripped him of academic belonging. Rohith wrote of his "unfulfilled dreams" and exhaustion from fighting systemic barriers, indicating hopelessness. Despite its brevity, the note conveyed his turmoil, with lines like "I always wanted to be a writer. A writer of science, like Carl Sagan," reflecting his thwarted aspirations. His call for others to continue the fight suggested lingering hope for change.

Critique of Institutional and Social Systems

Rohith's note was a sharp indictment of institutional and societal structures. He criticised the reduction of individuals to their caste identities, a process he felt was perpetuated by UoH's disciplinary measures, which the ASA alleged were biased against Dalit students. The note's reference to his "fatal accident" of birth challenged the university's failure to address caste discrimination. Rohith's mention of unpaid dues pointed to administrative neglect, which critics described as part of a dysfunctional grievance system. The university denied targeting Rohith, claiming administrative delays were routine.

Public and Academic Reception

After Rohith's death, the suicide note was widely circulated, becoming a catalyst for nationwide protests. Its eloquent critique of caste and institutional failures resonated with students and academics, who saw it as a call to action. Over 130 scholars globally condemned UoH's treatment of Rohith, citing the note as evidence of systemic casteism. The note's literary quality drew comparisons to Ambedkar's writings, with scholars describing it as a "profound philosophical statement" on caste oppression. It became a symbol of resistance, inspiring demands for the Rohith Vemula Act.

Legacy of the Note

The suicide note's impact extended beyond Rohith's death, shaping the narrative of caste discrimination in higher education. It was quoted in protests, academic discussions, and policy debates, with lines like "From shadows to the stars" adorning banners at UoH's 'Velivada.' The note's publication amplified calls for accountability, leading to investigations and reform proposals. Its emotional and intellectual weight made it a historical document, with supporters arguing that Rohith's death was an "institutional murder" driven by caste-based marginalisation.

Literary and Cultural Resonance

The note's poetic language and philosophical depth have cemented its place in India's anti-caste literary tradition, alongside works by Ambedkar and Dalit poets like Namdeo Dhasal. Its circulation inspired cultural expressions, including songs, documentaries, and plays, such as the 2017 documentary The Unseen Sequence, which explores

Rohith's life and legacy. The note's universal themes of alienation and resistance have resonated globally, with translations in multiple languages and discussions in international forums, reinforcing its role as a call for justice beyond India's borders.

Influence on Legal Reforms

The note's critique of institutional failures has directly influenced legal advocacy, notably the push for the Rohith Vemula Act. In 2025, Karnataka's draft Act cites the note's references to systemic marginalisation to justify provisions like mandatory anti-discrimination training for faculty. The Supreme Court's March 2025 directive to strengthen UGC regulations was partly inspired by the note's exposure of administrative neglect, with justices referencing its call for recognising individuals as "minds" rather than caste identities. These legal developments highlight the note's enduring impact on policy reform.

CHAPTER 10

January 17, 2016: The Day of Tragedy

The Circumstances of Rohith's Death

On 17 January 2016, Rohith Chakravarthi Vemula, a 26-year-old PhD scholar at the University of Hyderabad (UoH), was found dead in Room No. 207 of the New Research Scholars hostel, having died by suicide by hanging. The Gachibowli police were notified around 7:20 PM, with Rohith's body discovered by ASA friends after they grew concerned about his unresponsiveness. He was found with a rope around his neck, tied to a ceiling fan, alongside a suicide note. The note detailed his despair over caste-based marginalisation and institutional pressures, marking the day as a pivotal moment in India's discourse on caste discrimination.

Immediate Response at UoH

The discovery of Rohith's body triggered chaos and grief on the UoH campus. ASA members and students gathered at the hostel, mourning the loss of a friend and activist. The Joint Action Committee for Social Justice (JAC) mobilised, alleging that Rohith's death was an "institutional murder" driven by his suspension, hostel eviction, and stipend delays. UoH authorities notified the police, who faced resistance from students reluctant to allow immediate removal of the body, demanding accountability. The university expressed condolences but maintained that disciplinary actions were procedural, a claim contested as evasive.

Police and Medical Procedures

The Gachibowli police registered a case under Section 306 (abetment to suicide) and the SC/ST (Prevention of Atrocities) Act, based on complaints from Rohith's friends. A post-mortem at Osmania General Hospital on 18 January 2016 confirmed death by asphyxiation due to hanging, with no evidence of foul play. The police faced allegations of delaying medical intervention, with students claiming officers were obstructed by the crowd, though students argued they were protecting the scene for a thorough investigation. The police denied negligence, citing crowd control issues.

Allegations of Administrative Complicity

The JAC and ASA accused UoH's administration, particularly Vice-Chancellor P. Appa Rao, of contributing to Rohith's death through targeted disciplinary actions. They alleged that the suspension and eviction, following the August 2015 ABVP conflict, were caste-motivated and influenced by BJP MP Bandaru Dattatreya's letter to the MHRD. The university denied these allegations, asserting that the Executive Council's decisions were based on the proctorial board's findings. These conflicting narratives fuelled outrage, with students labelling the administration's response as callous.

Student Protests and Campus Unrest

Rohith's death sparked immediate protests at UoH, centred at 'Velivada.' On 18 January 2016, hundreds of students, led by the JAC, staged sit-ins, hunger strikes, and marches, demanding Appa Rao's resignation and the revocation of suspensions. The protests disrupted campus operations, with classes suspended and administrative buildings blockaded. Over 200 students gathered at the hostel, chanting "Justice for Rohith" and displaying banners with his suicide note excerpts. Faculty support grew, with SC/ST professors resigning from administrative posts, citing systemic casteism.

National Attention and Political Response

The tragedy gained national attention, with media outlets covering the events extensively. Political leaders, including Rahul Gandhi, visited UoH on 19 January 2016, criticising the BJP-led government for fostering caste-based discrimination, a charge the BJP rejected. Then-Union HRD Minister Smriti Irani argued in Parliament that Rohith's case was a disciplinary matter, not a caste issue, sparking opposition protests. The incident spurred calls for a Rohith Vemula Act to address caste discrimination in education, marking the day as a catalyst for a broader movement.

Media's Role in Amplifying the Tragedy

The extensive media coverage following 17 January 2016 played a crucial role in elevating Rohith's death to a national issue. Outlets like The Hindu and The Wire published his suicide note, sparking public outrage and drawing parallels to other Dalit student suicides. Television debates and social media campaigns, including hashtags like #JusticeForRohith, amplified the JAC's demands, with over 500,000 posts on social media by January 2017. This media attention pressured the government to address caste discrimination, though critics noted sensationalism in some reports risked overshadowing systemic issues.

Long-Term Impact on Campus Politics

Rohith's death reshaped UoH's political landscape, strengthening the ASA's influence and galvanising anti-caste activism. The 'Velivada' site became a permanent symbol of resistance, hosting annual commemorations that draw thousands. The protests led to a 2016 UGC policy mandating equal opportunity cells in universities, though implementation remains uneven. By 2025, the push for the Rohith Vemula Act reflects the enduring impact of 17 January 2016, with student unions citing the tragedy as a call for structural reform in higher education.

CHAPTER 11

Radhika Vemula: A Mother's Fight for Justice

A Grieving Mother's Emergence as an Advocate

Radhika Vemula, a 57-year-old single mother and tailor from Guntur, Andhra Pradesh, became a central figure in the fight for justice following her son Rohith's suicide on 17 January 2016 at the University of Hyderabad (UoH). Born into a Scheduled Caste (SC) Mala family but adopted by a Vaddera (OBC) household, Radhika faced caste-based discrimination throughout her life, shaping her resolve. His death, which she labelled an "institutional murder" due to UoH's punitive measures—suspension, hostel eviction, and stipend delays—propelled her into activism. With limited education and resources, Radhika's transformation into a national advocate for Dalit rights was remarkable, driven by a determination to hold authorities accountable.

Active Participation in Campus Protests

Radhika immersed herself in the protests at UoH, aligning with the ASA and the Joint Action Committee for Social Justice (JAC). She frequented the 'Velivada' protest site, addressing crowds with emotional speeches in Telugu about Rohith's aspirations and the institutional pressures he faced. Holding his photograph, she galvanised students, drawing hundreds to candlelight vigils and marches. Her visits to campuses like Jawaharlal Nehru University in February 2016 and events in Kerala in 2017 linked Rohith's case to broader struggles against caste discrimination, fostering a network of solidarity.

Pursuit of Legal Accountability

Radhika pursued justice through legal avenues, supporting a police case under Section 306 (abetment to suicide) and the SC/ST (Prevention of Atrocities) Act against Vice-Chancellor P. Appa Rao, BJP MP Bandaru Dattatreya, ABVP leader N. Susheel Kumar, and others. She alleged that Appa Rao's inaction and Dattatreya's political pressure escalated the conflict. The 2024 Telangana Police closure report, which absolved the accused and questioned Rohith's Dalit status, prompted her to demand a reinvestigation, leading to a commitment from Telangana's Chief Minister in May 2024. Her Supreme Court petition with Payal Tadvi's mother seeks measures to end caste discrimination in universities.

Embracing Buddhism as a Political Act

On 14 April 2016, Radhika and her son Raja converted to Buddhism during Ambedkar Jayanti, affirming their Dalit identity and aligning with Rohith's beliefs. The conversion was a response to attempts to classify them as Vaddera (OBC), which Radhika contested, supported by a Guntur collector's certification of her Mala heritage. She declared, "I am a Dalit. My son is a Dalit," rejecting the 2024 police report's findings. The act symbolised defiance of caste oppression and commitment to Ambedkarite principles, reinforcing her advocacy.

Confronting Character Assassination and Caste Disputes

Radhika faced scrutiny over her and Rohith's caste status, with the 2016 District Level Scrutiny Committee and 2017 Roopanwal Commission claiming she was Vaddera (OBC), dismissing SC/ST Act charges. She refuted allegations of fraudulently obtaining an SC certificate, supported by evidence of her Mala heritage. Statements by then-Union Minister Smriti Irani questioning Rohith's Dalit status were cited as character assassination. Radhika's 2024 rebuttals, including challenging the police report's DNA test suggestion, underscored her determination to defend her family's identity.

Building a National Movement for Justice

Radhika's advocacy evolved into a broader movement for Dalit rights. Her 2018 'Mothers for Nation Yatra' connected with families of caste discrimination victims like Payal Tadvi and Darshan Solanki. Her participation in the Bharat Jodo Yatra in 2022 and events like the 2017 Elgaar Parishad highlighted her call for a Rohith Vemula Act. Her 2025 Bengaluru speech emphasised protective legislation, inspiring policy discussions and establishing her as a respected voice in the fight against caste oppression.

Role in Shaping Public Discourse

Radhika's public appearances, often alongside activists like Jignesh Mevani, have shaped India's discourse on caste and education. Her speeches, blending personal grief with calls for systemic change, have been covered extensively, with over 1,000 news articles by 2025 citing her advocacy. Her rejection of the 2024 police report sparked nationwide protests, with student unions adopting her slogan,

"Rohith's fight is our fight." Her ability to mobilize diverse groups, including non-Dalit allies, has broadened the anti-caste movement, making her a pivotal figure in public consciousness.

Influence on Legislative Advocacy

Radhika's campaign has directly influenced legislative efforts, particularly the Rohith Vemula Act. Her 2025 meetings with Karnataka ministers helped shape the draft Act's provisions, including compensation for discrimination victims and mandatory anti-caste training. The Supreme Court's March 2025 directive to strengthen UGC regulations cited her petition, emphasising her role in legal reform. Her advocacy for reinvestigating Rohith's case, backed by Telangana's 2024 commitment, underscores her impact on ensuring accountability, cementing her legacy as a catalyst for change.

CHAPTER 12

The Caste Controversy: Was Rohith Dalit?

Genesis of the Caste Identity Dispute

The question of whether Rohith Chakravarthi Vemula belonged to the Scheduled Caste (SC) Mala community or the Other Backward Classes (OBC) Vaddera community became a contentious issue following his suicide on 17 January 2016 at the University of Hyderabad (UoH). This dispute was pivotal, impacting the applicability of the SC/ST (Prevention of Atrocities) Act in the case against UoH Vice-Chancellor P. Appa Rao, BJP MP Bandaru Dattatreya, and others. It arose from conflicting claims about Rohith's family background, with his mother, Radhika Vemula, asserting her Mala identity, while official inquiries emphasised his father's Vaddera caste. Radhika's adoption by a Vaddera family complicated matters, raising questions about birth, upbringing, and legal caste status. The controversy became a focal point for debates on caste identity, systemic discrimination, and reservation politics, shaping the justice movement sparked by Rohith's death.

Radhika Vemula's Assertion of Mala Identity

Radhika Vemula's claim that she and her children, including Rohith, were Mala was central to their identity.

Born in 1962 to a Mala family in Guntur, Andhra Pradesh, Radhika was adopted at age five by a Vaddera woman, Anjani Devi, after economic hardship. She faced caste-based discrimination in the Vaddera household, shaping her and Rohith's Dalit identity. Married at 14 to V. Naga Mani Kumar, a Vaddera, in an arranged marriage that concealed her Mala origins, Radhika separated due to domestic violence, raising Rohith, Raja, and Nileema in a Mala-dominated neighbourhood. In 1992, she obtained an SC certificate classifying them as Mala, affirmed by Guntur District Collector Kantilal Dande in 2016. Radhika insisted Rohith lived as a Dalit, facing prejudice and embracing this identity through his ASA activism, declaring in 2024, "I am a Dalit. My son is a Dalit, as I brought him up."

Official Inquiries and Contradictory Classifications

Official inquiries challenged Radhika's claims, driven by legal and political motives. In February 2016, the Guntur District Level Scrutiny Committee, prompted by Vaddera complaints and BJP leaders, questioned her SC certificate. Its July 2016 report classified Radhika and her children as Vaddera, citing her adoption and marriage to Mani Kumar, despite her Mala birth. The 2017 Roopanwal Commission endorsed this, concluding Rohith was not Dalit, dismissing SC/ST Act charges. Radhika and Raja countered that Mani Kumar, estranged since Rohith's childhood, had no role in their upbringing. The National Commission for Scheduled Castes' 2016 investigation upheld Radhika's Mala status, and the Hyderabad High Court refused to stay the SC/ST Act charges, noting evidence of Rohith's Dalit identity. These contradictions fuelled allegations of political orchestration by the BJP-led government to protect the accused.

Legal and Social Ramifications

The caste dispute impacted the SC/ST Act's applicability, which requires the victim to be SC/ST and the accused non-SC/ST. Radhika's legal team cited a 2012 Supreme Court ruling allowing children of inter-caste marriages to claim the mother's caste if raised in her community, arguing Rohith's Mala upbringing and SC certificate qualified him as Dalit. The dispute raised social questions about patriarchal bias in prioritising Mani Kumar's caste. Dalit activists affirmed Rohith's Mala identity, with community leaders stating he was embraced as Dalit. Feminist scholars criticised the state's dismissal of Radhika's lived experience, highlighting gender and caste inequities. The controversy underscored the tension between legal caste definitions and social realities in inter-caste families.

Political Exploitation and Media Narratives

The caste controversy was politicised, with media amplifying competing narratives. In 2016, then-Union HRD Minister Smriti Irani claimed Rohith was not Dalit, citing early police findings, a stance opposition leaders condemned as deflecting from institutional casteism. BJP leaders supported the Vaddera classification, arguing the SC/ST Act charges were baseless, which Radhika called "character assassination." Media outlets critiqued the patriarchal bias in official reports, while some noted inconclusive police probes into Radhika's SC certificate. The polarised coverage fuelled debate, with Dalit activists accusing the government of erasing Rohith's identity, while BJP supporters defended caste verification as a legal necessity.

Lasting Impact on the Justice Movement

The caste controversy energised and complicated the justice movement. Radhika's assertion of her Mala identity, supported by the NCSC and community, reinforced the narrative that Rohith's death was a caste atrocity, sustaining protests and demands for a Rohith Vemula Act. However, official Vaddera classifications provided legal leverage to the accused, culminating in the 2024 Telangana Police closure report, which Radhika challenged, securing a reinvestigation. The dispute sparked discussions on caste identity, with activists arguing Rohith's self-identification as Dalit should supersede bureaucratic classifications, highlighting challenges in caste verification and its impact on justice.

Legal Precedents on Caste Identity

The caste dispute aligns with evolving legal precedents in India, where courts have increasingly recognised lived experience in determining caste status. The Supreme Court's 2012 Rameshbhai Dabhai Naika ruling, cited by Radhika's legal team, emphasises upbringing over patrilineal caste, a principle reaffirmed in 2023 cases allowing children of inter-caste marriages to claim SC status based on community acceptance. These precedents support Radhika's claim, as Rohith's Mala upbringing and SC certificate were verified by Guntur authorities, challenging the Scrutiny Committee's focus on her adoptive family. This legal framework underscores the controversy's significance in shaping caste jurisprudence.

Socio-Cultural Implications

The controversy reflects broader socio-cultural tensions in India's caste system, where identity is both fluid and rigidly policed. Rohith's activism and Radhika's advocacy highlight how Dalit self-identification often clashes with state mechanisms, as seen in similar disputes involving Payal Tadvi's tribal status. The emphasis on Mani Kumar's caste perpetuates patriarchal norms, ignoring Radhika's role as the primary caregiver. By 2025, Dalit movements have leveraged the controversy to advocate for community-driven caste recognition, influencing debates on the Rohith Vemula Act, which seeks to protect SC/ST students regardless of contested classifications.

CHAPTER 13

Telangana Police Closure Report (2024)

Background and Filing of the Closure Report

On 21 March 2024, the Telangana Police, under the Cyberabad Commissionerate, filed a closure report in the Rohith Vemula suicide case with the LB Nagar Sessions Court, concluding its investigation into his 17 January 2016 death. Prepared by Assistant Commissioner of Police C.H. Sreekanth, the report was based on a 2016 case under Section 306 (abetment to suicide) and the SC/ST (Prevention of Atrocities) Act. Finalised before November 2023 but submitted eight years later, its release, 10 days before Telangana's Lok Sabha elections on 13 May 2024, under a Congress-led government, sparked controversy. The report's findings on Rohith's caste and exoneration of key figures ignited public and familial backlash, highlighting ongoing tensions over caste discrimination in academia.

Key Findings on Caste Identity

The closure report claimed Rohith was not a Dalit, asserting he belonged to the Vaddera (OBC) community, based on his father's caste and Radhika Vemula's adoption by a Vaddera family. It alleged Radhika obtained an SC certificate fraudulently, suggesting Rohith's fear of exposure drove his suicide. Radhika rejected these claims, citing her 1992 SC certificate and a 2016 Guntur District Collector's report affirming her Mala status. She accused the police of fabricating the caste narrative to undermine the SC/ST Act charges, calling the report "full of lies" at a 4 May 2024 press conference. The report's reliance on the 2016 Scrutiny Committee's Vaddera classification, despite contradictory NCSC findings, fuelled allegations of bias.

Exoneration of Accused Individuals

The report absolved UoH Vice-Chancellor P. Appa Rao, BJP MP Bandaru Dattatreya, BJP MLC N. Ramachander Rao, ABVP leader N. Susheel Kumar, and then-Union HRD Minister Smriti Irani, citing insufficient evidence for abetment. It argued that the university's disciplinary actions—suspending and evicting Rohith and four ASA members—were within UoH statutes, with Appa Rao taking a "lenient view" by reducing expulsion to hostel restrictions. It claimed Dattatreya's 2015 MHRD letter had no direct influence, as proctorial board and Executive Council members reported no awareness of it. The ASA and JAC alleged a cover-up, claiming political pressure protected the accused, which Dattatreya and Appa Rao denied.

Allegations of Investigative Bias

Critics accused the report of bias for focusing on Rohith's caste rather than his death's circumstances. The ASA and Raja Vemula argued that the police avoided investigating whether university harassment drove Rohith to suicide, dedicating over 30 pages to disputing his Dalit identity. Claims that Rohith was not studious and had "violent tendencies" based on ABVP testimonies were refuted by Radhika, citing his 70% MSc score. The report's timing under a Congress government led to allegations of collusion with BJP narratives, though DGP Ravi Gupta clarified it was prepared under the previous BRS government. Critics labelled the report a "whitewash" to protect powerful figures.

Public and Familial Backlash

The report triggered outrage, with Radhika, Raja, and the ASA condemning its findings. On 3 May 2024, UoH students protested, demanding a fresh probe, joined by faculty and groups like the SFI, which called the report an "exercise in irony." Radhika's press conference rejected the caste and academic claims, asserting her Dalit identity. Raja challenged the police's caste determination authority, planning a court protest petition. Their meeting with Chief Minister A. Revanth Reddy on 4 May 2024 secured a reinvestigation commitment, reflecting public pressure. The backlash underscored the report's failure to address institutional casteism, reigniting justice demands.

Political Context and Broader Implications

The report's release during the 2024 election campaign raised questions of political motives. The Congress, which supported the 'Justice for Rohith' campaign, faced criticism for the report's alignment with BJP narratives. The reinvestigation commitment mitigated electoral damage while addressing public demands. The report highlighted flaws in caste verification and police investigations, relying on contested findings while ignoring NCSC affirmations. It strengthened calls for a Rohith Vemula Act, with Radhika and the ASA advocating for protections against caste discrimination, emphasising the case's role in anti-caste movements.

Investigative Flaws and Accountability Gaps

The closure report's investigative flaws, such as its reliance on ABVP testimonies and failure to probe harassment, reflect broader issues in handling caste-related cases. A 2025 report by the National Campaign on Dalit Human Rights noted that 70% of SC/ST Act cases in Telangana face delays or closure due to biased investigations, as seen in Rohith's case. The Supreme Court's March 2025 directive to strengthen UGC regulations, prompted by Radhika's petition, aims to address such gaps, but activists argue for independent oversight to ensure impartiality, a demand fueled by the report's backlash.

National Policy Debates

The closure report's controversy has spurred national debates on caste discrimination in education. The proposed Rohith Vemula Act, backed by Karnataka's 2025 draft, includes provisions for independent probes into caste-related complaints, inspired by Rohith's case. Congress leaders like Rahul Gandhi have cited the report's flaws to push for legislative reforms, with 2025 campaigns emphasising the need for systemic change. The report's failure to address institutional accountability has galvanised student unions, with over 50 universities holding solidarity protests by May 2024, reinforcing the case's impact on policy advocacy.

CHAPTER 14

Reopening the Investigation

Catalyst for Reopening the Case

The decision to reopen the investigation into Rohith Vemula's suicide, announced on 4 May 2024 by the Telangana Police, responded to widespread outrage over the 21 March 2024 closure report. The report, which claimed Rohith was not a Dalit and absolved figures like UoH Vice-Chancellor P. Appa Rao and BJP MP Bandaru Dattatreya, was criticised by Rohith's family, the Ambedkar Students' Association (ASA), and progressive groups. Its release, 10 days before Telangana's Lok Sabha elections on 13 May 2024, under a Congress-led government, intensified scrutiny, given Congress's prior support for the 'Justice for Rohith' campaign. Radhika Vemula's advocacy and student protests drove the reversal, marking a significant moment in the eight-year legal battle over caste-based discrimination in academia.

Radhika Vemula's Advocacy and Political Engagement

Radhika Vemula was pivotal in pressuring authorities. On 3 May 2024, she denounced the closure report as "full of lies" for questioning Rohith's Scheduled Caste (SC) Mala identity and alleging he feared exposure of a fabricated caste certificate. She cited her 1992 SC certificate and a

2016 Guntur District Collector's report affirming her Mala status. On 4 May 2024, Radhika and her son Raja met Telangana Chief Minister A. Revanth Reddy, presenting a memorandum demanding a reinvestigation. Reddy, whose Congress party pledged a Rohith Vemula Act in 2023, assured a transparent probe, leading to the police's announcement. Radhika's advocacy, built on her 'Mothers for Nation Yatra' and engagements with Congress leaders like Rahul Gandhi, framed Rohith's death as an institutional failure rooted in casteism.

Telangana Police's Response and Legal Steps

The Telangana Police, led by Director General of Police Ravi Gupta, announced further investigation on 4 May 2024, citing "doubts expressed by the mother and others." Gupta clarified that the closure report, prepared before November 2023 under the Bharat Rashtra Samithi government, was filed on 21 March 2024. The police planned to file a petition in the LB Nagar Sessions Court under Section 173(8) of the Criminal Procedure Code, seeking permission for additional inquiries. The reinvestigation aimed to address concerns about the report's focus on Rohith's caste rather than alleged harassment, though its scope remained undisclosed. The ASA and JAC welcomed the decision but expressed scepticism, alleging the initial report reflected bias by relying on ABVP testimonies and contested caste findings.

Student Protests and Public Outcry

The closure report sparked immediate protests at UoH, with over 200 students gathering on 3 May 2024 at the North Shopping Complex, demanding a fresh probe. Organised by the ASA and supported by the Students'

Federation of India and other groups, the protests condemned the report's caste claims and exoneration of the accused, targeting the BJP and former HRD Minister Smriti Irani. Faculty, including SC/ST professors who resigned administrative posts in 2016, joined, amplifying demands for accountability. Public outcry extended beyond UoH, with intellectuals labelling the report a "whitewash." The protests and Radhika's media appearances pressured the Congress government, contributing to the reinvestigation commitment.

Political Dynamics and Allegations of Collusion

The report's release during the 2024 election campaign intensified allegations of political manipulation. The Congress, in power in Telangana since December 2023, faced criticism for the report's alignment with BJP narratives, despite its 2016 support for Rohith's cause. TPCC vice-president G. Niranjan urged a re-enquiry, distancing the party from the police's findings. The ASA alleged a nexus between the police, ABVP, and RSS, pointing to the report's reliance on ABVP testimonies. BJP leaders defended the report, accusing Congress of politicising Rohith's death, while Radhika rejected these claims as deflections. The reinvestigation was seen as Congress's attempt to mitigate electoral damage while addressing public demands.

Broader Implications for Justice and Caste Discourse

The reinvestigation reaffirmed Rohith's case as central to highlighting institutional casteism. It offered hope for a probe into whether UoH's disciplinary actions, political pressures, or caste discrimination contributed to Rohith's suicide. It spotlighted flaws in caste verification, as the police's Vaddera finding contrasted with the NCSC's Mala affirmation, raising questions about legal standards for inter-caste families. The case's revival strengthened calls for a Rohith Vemula Act, with Radhika and the ASA advocating for protections against discrimination. The reinvestigation, while a victory, underscored challenges in politically charged cases, with outcomes hinging on the court's response and the probe's transparency.

Role of Social Media in Mobilization

Social media played a crucial role in amplifying the backlash against the closure report, with hashtags like #JusticeForRohith trending on social media platforms , garnering over 300,000 posts by May 2024. Student unions and activists used social media to coordinate protests and share Radhika's press conference, reaching millions and pressuring the Telangana government. The rapid spread of information online, including excerpts from Rohith's suicide note, rekindled public outrage, ensuring the case remained a national issue. This digital mobilisation, echoing the 2016 protests, highlighted social media's power in sustaining anti-caste movements and influencing policy responses.

Impact on National Anti-Caste Movements

The reinvestigation invigorated national anti-caste movements, with over 50 universities holding solidarity protests by May 2024. The case's revival inspired legislative advocacy, notably Karnataka's 2025 draft Rohith Vemula Act, which proposes penalties for caste-based discrimination. Radhika's collaboration with activists like Jignesh Mevani and families of other victims, such as Payal Tadvi, strengthened a coalition pushing for systemic reform. The Supreme Court's 2025 directive to bolster UGC regulations, citing Rohith's case, underscored its influence on national efforts to address caste inequities in education, cementing its legacy in the anti-caste struggle.

CHAPTER 15

The Role of University Authorities

Leadership and Administrative Structure at UoH

The University of Hyderabad (UoH), established in 1974, was governed by a hierarchy led by Vice-Chancellor P. Appa Rao, appointed in September 2015, during the events surrounding Rohith Vemula's suicide in January 2016. Appa Rao held executive authority, supported by the Executive Council (EC), the university's highest decision-making body, comprising faculty, external experts, and officers like the Registrar. Proctorial boards handled student conduct inquiries, reporting to the EC. With over 5,000 students, including significant SC/ST and OBC representation, UoH's academic excellence coexisted with caste-related tensions, evident in prior incidents like the 2002 rustication of 10 Dalit students and the 2013 suicides of Dalit scholars Pulyala Raju and Madari Venkatesh, which the ASA linked to administrative bias.

Handling of the August 2015 ASA-ABVP Conflict

The authorities' response to the August 2015 conflict between the ASA and ABVP was critical. On 3 August 2015, the ASA protested the ABVP's disruption of a documentary screening at Delhi University, leading to an altercation where ABVP leader N. Susheel Kumar claimed assault by ASA members, including Rohith. The proctorial board, chaired by Dean Alok Pandey, concluded on 12 August 2015 that no assault occurred but recommended disciplinary action for a breach of discipline. The ASA alleged a rushed and biased inquiry, which the university denied, asserting fairness. The EC, under Appa Rao, suspended Rohith and four others—Dontha Prashanth, Vijay Kumar, Seshu Chemudugunta, and Vinod Kumar—in September 2015, escalating to hostel evictions and campus restrictions in December 2015.

Allegations of Caste-Based Bias in Disciplinary Actions

The ASA accused Appa Rao of caste-based bias, calling the suspensions and evictions a "social boycott" unprecedented at UoH, barring students from hostels, administrative buildings, and mess facilities. Critics argued the EC ignored the proctorial board's no-assault finding, failing to consider the students' Dalit identities. The JAC claimed Appa Rao's history, including alleged anti-Dalit actions in 2002, indicated bias. UoH authorities denied these allegations, stating the EC's decisions followed norms, with Registrar M. Sudhakar asserting transparency. The controversy intensified perceptions of institutional casteism, fuelling protests after Rohith's death.

Response to Rohith's December 2015 Letter

Rohith's 18 December 2015 letter to Appa Rao, sarcastically requesting "10 mg of Sodium Azide" and a rope for Dalit students, tested the authorities' responsiveness. Emailed and copied to faculty, it expressed frustration over caste discrimination and disciplinary actions. The JAC and ASA alleged Appa Rao ignored it, failing to address systemic casteism, with critics noting administrative inaction. UoH countered that the letter was not formally submitted through grievance channels, and Appa Rao was preoccupied with disciplinary reviews. The lack of response was cited as evidence of indifference, contributing to Rohith's despair, as reflected in his suicide note.

Actions Following Rohith's Suicide

After Rohith's suicide on 17 January 2016, UoH faced scrutiny. Appa Rao issued condolences on 18 January 2016 but defended the disciplinary actions, enraging students and the JAC, who demanded his resignation. Allegations of delaying police and medical response surfaced, with the ASA claiming obstruction, though UoH attributed delays to student protests. On 22 January 2016, Appa Rao took leave, citing health issues, as protests escalated. The EC appointed Pro-Vice-Chancellor Vipin Srivastava as acting Vice-Chancellor, but protests continued. An MHRD panel in February 2016 found UoH mishandled the disciplinary process, recommending reforms, which the university claimed to address internally.

Long-Term Implications and Accountability

UoH's role had lasting implications for institutional accountability. The 2024 Telangana Police closure report absolved Appa Rao, citing his "lenient" reduction of expulsion, a claim the ASA disputed, noting the boycott's severity. Radhika accused the authorities of colluding with political figures, which Appa Rao denied. The MHRD panel's findings highlighted systemic failures, including inadequate grievance systems. The case spurred demands for a Rohith Vemula Act, with Radhika and the ASA advocating for protections against caste discrimination, emphasising the need for administrative reforms to ensure equity in higher education.

Historical Caste-Related Incidents at UoH

UoH's history of caste-related incidents contextualises the 2015 events. The 2002 rustication of 10 Dalit students for protesting administrative bias and the 2013 suicides of Pulyala Raju and Madari Venkatesh, linked by the ASA to caste discrimination, reveal a pattern of institutional neglect. These incidents, alongside Rohith's case, indicate systemic issues, with SC/ST students facing disproportionate disciplinary actions, as noted in a 2021 UGC report showing 60% of suspensions in central universities targeting reserved category students. This history underscores the need for structural reforms to address casteism at UoH.

2025 UGC Regulatory Changes

The Supreme Court's March 2025 directive to strengthen UGC anti-discrimination regulations, prompted by Radhika's petition, marked a response to UoH's failures. The UGC's 2025 draft regulations propose mandatory anti-caste training and independent grievance cells, addressing issues highlighted by Rohith's case. Karnataka's draft Rohith Vemula Act, supported by Rahul Gandhi in April 2025, includes provisions holding administrators accountable for caste-based discrimination, reflecting UoH's role in galvanising reform. These changes aim to prevent future tragedies, though activists stress enforcement remains critical to ensuring accountability.

CHAPTER 16

Political Involvement: Smriti Irani and Bandaru Dattatreya

Bandaru Dattatreya's Letter to the MHRD

The political involvement in the Rohith Vemula case began with a letter dated 17 August 2015 from Bandaru Dattatreya, then Union Minister of State for Labour and Employment and Secunderabad MP, to Smriti Irani, the Union Minister for Human Resource Development (MHRD). Written on ministerial letterhead, the letter addressed concerns raised by N. Susheel Kumar, the Akhil Bharatiya Vidyarthi Parishad (ABVP) president at the University of Hyderabad (UoH), following an August 2015 clash with the Ambedkar Students' Association (ASA). Dattatreya described UoH as a hub of "casteist, extremist, and anti-national politics," citing the ASA's protest against the ABVP's disruption of a documentary screening as evidence of "anti-social activities." He urged Irani to act against the ASA, alleging the university administration was unresponsive. The letter, outside Dattatreya's labour portfolio, prompted the MHRD to send five follow-up letters to UoH between September and November 2015, inquiring about disciplinary actions. The ASA and Radhika Vemula alleged that Dattatreya's letter pressured UoH to suspend and evict Rohith and four other ASA members, a claim Dattatreya denied, stating he was forwarding a constituent's concerns.

MHRD's Follow-Up and Alleged Influence

The MHRD, under Smriti Irani, responded swiftly, sending communications to UoH's Vice-Chancellor P. Appa Rao on 3 September, 24 September, 20 October, 2 November, and 19 November 2015, pressing for updates on actions against the ASA members. The ASA and the Joint Action Committee for Social Justice (JAC) alleged these letters demonstrated undue ministerial interference, influencing UoH's decision to suspend and evict the five students, despite the proctorial board finding no assault. Irani denied direct influence, stating in January 2016 that the MHRD only forwarded complaints and that the university's Executive Council (EC), appointed under the UPA government, acted independently. Critics argued that the MHRD's persistent inquiries bypassed standard procedures, pressuring UoH to target Dalit students, exacerbating the tensions that led to Rohith's suicide.

Smriti Irani's Public Statements Post-Suicide

Following Rohith's suicide on 17 January 2016, Smriti Irani faced criticism for her handling of the case. In a January 2016 press conference, she rejected allegations of caste-based discrimination, asserting that Rohith's death was not a "Dalit versus non-Dalit issue" and that Susheel Kumar was OBC. She claimed Rohith's suicide note did not blame any minister or official, accusing opposition parties of politicising the tragedy. In a February 2016 Lok Sabha speech, Irani stated no doctor was allowed near Rohith's body to revive him, a claim contradicted by UoH's duty doctor, who confirmed examining the body and declaring death within minutes. Radhika Vemula accused Irani of "blatant lies," particularly for questioning Rohith's Dalit status and branding him "anti-national," claims Irani defended as factual, escalating public outrage.

Allegations of Political Pressure and Abetment

The ASA, JAC, and Radhika alleged that Dattatreya and Irani's actions constituted political pressure that abetted Rohith's suicide. A January 2016 police case under Section 306 (abetment to suicide) and the SC/ST (Prevention of Atrocities) Act named Dattatreya, Irani, Appa Rao, Susheel Kumar, and BJP MLC N. Ramachander Rao, citing Dattatreya's letter and MHRD follow-ups as catalysts for UoH's punitive measures. The JAC claimed Dattatreya, influenced by the ABVP and RSS, misrepresented the ASA to target Dalit students. Irani was accused of exacerbating the situation by endorsing the MHRD's inquiries and misrepresenting facts. Both denied abetment, with Dattatreya claiming his letter addressed campus unrest and Irani insisting the EC acted independently. The 2024 Telangana Police closure report absolved both, citing no evidence, a finding Radhika and the ASA rejected as biased.

Political Fallout and Opposition Response

The involvement of Irani and Dattatreya sparked a backlash, with opposition parties accusing the BJP of anti-Dalit policies. Rahul Gandhi visited UoH twice in January 2016, condemning the BJP's role, a move Irani criticised as politicisation. In February 2016, opposition leaders announced privilege motions against Irani in Parliament, accusing her of misleading statements about Rohith's case. Congress MP Hanumantha Rao accused Irani of twisting his 2014 letter about prior Dalit suicides at UoH to deflect blame. The opposition's actions escalated the case into a national debate, with protests spreading to JNU and other universities, amplifying demands for accountability and highlighting the political dimensions of Rohith's death.

Long-Term Implications for Political Accountability

The involvement of Irani and Dattatreya had lasting implications for political accountability and caste discourse. A 2016 MHRD panel criticised UoH's disciplinary process, indirectly pointing to MHRD's pressure, though no action was taken against Irani or Dattatreya. The 2024 closure report's exoneration reignited accusations of a cover-up, with Radhika alleging political influence shielded them. The case highlighted the dangers of ministerial overreach in academia, undermining university autonomy and exacerbating caste tensions. It fuelled demands for the Rohith Vemula Act, with activists urging legislation to prevent political targeting of marginalised students, a proposal gaining traction in 2024.

Political Climate of 2015–2016

The political climate of 2015–2016, marked by rising tensions over "anti-national" narratives, shaped the Rohith Vemula case. The BJP-led government's crackdowns on student activism, notably at JNU with Kanhaiya Kumar's arrest in February 2016, paralleled the targeting of ASA's activism as "anti-national." Dattatreya's letter reflected this narrative, aligning with ABVP's agenda to curb Left and Dalit student movements. The MHRD's swift response under Irani, amidst a broader push to control university autonomy, intensified perceptions of political interference. This climate, as noted in 2025 analyses, contextualises the case as part of a pattern of suppressing dissent, with

Rohith's death exposing the intersection of caste and political agendas.

Closure Report's Impact on Accountability

The 2024 closure report's exoneration of Irani and Dattatreya, despite the MHRD's documented follow-ups, underscored gaps in political accountability. The report's focus on Rohith's caste rather than political pressure, as criticised by the ASA in May 2024, reignited demands for independent probes into ministerial roles. The Supreme Court's 2025 directive to strengthen UGC regulations, citing political interference in cases like Rohith's, highlighted the need for mechanisms to prevent such overreach. Radhika's advocacy, linking the report's flaws to Irani's 2016 statements, sustained pressure for accountability, influencing 2025 legislative debates on the Rohith Vemula Act.

CHAPTER 17

Nationwide Protests: A Movement Ignited

Outbreak of Protests at UoH

Rohith Vemula's suicide on 17 January 2016 at the University of Hyderabad (UoH) triggered an immediate response on campus, marking the start of a nationwide movement against caste discrimination. Within hours, hundreds of students, led by the Ambedkar Students' Association (ASA) and the Joint Action Committee for Social Justice (JAC), gathered at the 'Velivada' protest site—a tent near the North Shopping Complex where Rohith and four suspended ASA members had lived after their hostel eviction. Starting 18 January 2016, sit-ins, candlelight vigils, and marches, involving over 200 students, blockaded administrative buildings, demanding Vice-Chancellor P. Appa Rao's resignation. The JAC accused the university of an "institutional murder," citing the suspension, eviction, and stipend delays as caste-driven. Slogans like "Justice for Rohith" and banners with his suicide note's lines, such as "My birth is my fatal accident," became rallying cries, making UoH the epicentre of the movement.

Spread to Other Universities and Cities

The protests spread rapidly, igniting solidarity across Indian universities and cities. By 19 January 2016, students at Jawaharlal Nehru University (JNU), Jadavpur University, IIT Bombay, and Osmania University organised marches and seminars condemning casteism. JNU's student union held a vigil on 19 January, attended by over 500 students, linking Rohith's death to systemic discrimination. In Mumbai, TISS students protested on 20 January, demanding a national law to protect SC/ST students, while Delhi University's Ambedkarite groups rallied at the MHRD office, accusing Smriti Irani of complicity. Urban protests erupted in Chennai, Bengaluru, and Lucknow, with thousands joining candle marches. The All India Students' Association (AISA) coordinated a Delhi rally on 1 February 2016, facing police baton charges, highlighting state resistance. The protests' scale, involving diverse groups, underscored Rohith's case as a symbol of institutional injustice.

Political Engagement and Opposition Support

The protests drew opposition party engagement, accusing the BJP of anti-Dalit policies. Rahul Gandhi visited UoH on 19 and 30 January 2016, addressing over 1,000 students and pledging a Rohith Vemula Act, a commitment reiterated in 2024. CPI(M) leader Sitaram Yechury joined JNU protests on 21 January, condemning the MHRD's role, while AAP's Arvind Kejriwal met Radhika Vemula on 23 January, promising legal support. JD(U)'s Nitish Kumar criticised the BJP during a Patna rally on 25 January, attended by 2,000 students. The ASA alleged BJP figures like Bandaru Dattatreya pressured UoH, a claim Dattatreya denied. The BJP accused the opposition of politicising the tragedy, with Irani alleging electoral motives. This polarisation fuelled the protests' visibility.

Faculty and Academic Community Response

UoH faculty and scholars nationwide rallied behind the cause. On 20 January 2016, 10 SC/ST professors resigned from administrative posts, citing systemic casteism and Appa Rao's inaction. Faculty like T. T. Sreekumar joined 'Velivada,' linking Rohith's death to Dalit struggles. Over 130 global scholars from Harvard, Oxford, and SOAS signed a January 2016 letter condemning UoH's "social boycott" of ASA members. The Indian People's Tribunal's February 2016 report concluded UoH's actions reflected institutional casteism, endorsed by scholars like Anand Teltumbde. Faculty resignations and statements challenged UoH's claim that disciplinary actions were routine, lending intellectual weight to the protests.

Demands for Systemic Reform

The protests demanded a Rohith Vemula Act to address caste discrimination. The JAC's 18 January 2016 memorandum called for Appa Rao's dismissal, suspension revocations, and a national law. JNU, TISS, and IIT Bombay students drafted legislative frameworks, proposing caste sensitisation and grievance cells. Protesters targeted Dattatreya's MHRD letter and Irani's follow-ups as evidence of interference. Radhika Vemula urged students on 24 January 2016 to fight for a "Rohith Act," a call gaining traction in 2024 when Karnataka and Telangana committed to drafting such a law. These demands transformed the protests into a broader anti-caste movement, influencing policy and academic reforms.

Legacy and Continued Activism

The protests left a lasting legacy, sustaining activism beyond 2016. 'Velivada' became a permanent symbol of Dalit resistance, hosting annual commemorations, with 2025 protests demanding the Rohith Vemula Act. The movement inspired campaigns like the 2019 Payal Tadvi protests, with Radhika joining Tadvi's mother to petition the Supreme Court. Estimated at over 2,000 participants across 20 cities by 30 January 2016, the protests set a precedent for student-led activism. The 2024 closure report reignited protests, with the ASA accusing the state of undermining Rohith's Dalit identity. The movement reshaped India's discourse on caste in education, fostering a sustained push for justice.

Role of Dalit Organisations

Dalit organisations, such as the Mala Mahanadu and Bhim Army, amplified the protests, mobilising thousands in Andhra Pradesh and Uttar Pradesh. The Mala Mahanadu's 2016 rallies in Guntur, attended by over 3,000, affirmed Rohith's Mala identity, countering the Scrutiny Committee's Vaddera claim. Bhim Army's Delhi protests in February 2016 linked Rohith's case to broader Dalit rights, influencing 2025 campaigns for the Rohith Vemula Act. These groups' grassroots efforts, as noted in 2024 reports, ensured the movement's longevity, connecting campus activism to community struggles and strengthening the anti-caste narrative.

Global Academic Solidarity

The protests garnered global academic support, extending their impact. Beyond the 130-scholar letter, international forums like the 2016 American Anthropological

Association conference discussed Rohith's case, with panels on caste in education. UK and US student unions, including Oxford's Dalit Solidarity Network, held vigils in February 2016, urging Indian universities to adopt anti-discrimination policies. This solidarity, documented in 2025 analyses, pressured UoH and the MHRD, contributing to the 2016 MHRD panel's critique of disciplinary processes and reinforcing the movement's call for systemic reform on a global stage.

CHAPTER 18

The Rohith Vemula Act: A Proposed Solution

Emergence of the Rohith Vemula Act Proposal

Rohith Vemula's suicide on 17 January 2016 at the University of Hyderabad (UoH) sparked a movement highlighting caste-based discrimination in Indian higher education. The call for a "Rohith Vemula Act" emerged as a legislative solution to protect marginalised students, particularly from Scheduled Castes (SC), Scheduled Tribes (ST), Other Backward Classes (OBC), and minorities. Proposed by the Joint Action Committee for Social Justice (JAC) and the Ambedkar Students' Association (ASA) in a January 2016 memorandum to the Ministry of Human Resource Development (MHRD), the Act aimed to prevent caste discrimination, inspired by Rohith's suicide note critiquing caste oppression and institutional failures. The proposal gained traction as protests spread to universities like JNU, TISS, and IIT Bombay, with activists and academics advocating for a legal framework to ensure equity and dignity in academia.

Core Objectives and Proposed Provisions

The Rohith Vemula Act seeks to prevent caste-based discrimination, exclusion, and harassment in educational institutions. Its objectives include safeguarding the right to education and dignity for SC, ST, OBC, and minority students, establishing institutional accountability, and providing grievance redressal mechanisms. Karnataka's 2025 draft, titled the Karnataka Rohith Vemula (Prevention of Exclusion or Injustice) (Right to Education and Dignity) Bill, proposes up to one year's imprisonment and a ₹10000 fine for individuals discriminating against marginalised students, ₹1 lakh compensation for victims, and penalties for institutional heads, including loss of government grants for non-compliant institutions. The bill aims to criminalise denial of admission or amenities based on caste, mandate caste sensitisation programmes, and establish independent complaint cells, addressing Rohith's experience of suspension, eviction, and stipend delays, which the JAC labelled a "social boycott."

Political Support and Congress's Commitment

The Congress party championed the Rohith Vemula Act, integrating it into its social justice agenda. In February 2023, Congress resolved to enact the Act nationally if elected, aiming to protect marginalised students. Congress General Secretary K.C. Venugopal reiterated this in May 2024, promising a national law post the Telangana Police closure report. Rahul Gandhi urged Congress-ruled states—Karnataka, Telangana, and Himachal Pradesh—on 16 April 2025 to expedite the Act, invoking the legacies of Dr. B.R. Ambedkar, Rohith Vemula, Payal Tadvi, and Darshan Solanki, whose deaths he called "murders" due to caste oppression. Karnataka Chief Minister Siddaramaiah responded on 19 April 2025, directing his legal team to draft the bill, pledging swift enactment to honour Rohith's dream of dignity. Congress's advocacy aimed to consolidate

SC, ST, and OBC support, though the BJP accused it of politicising the issue.

Karnataka's Draft Bill and Legislative Process

Karnataka led the drafting of the Rohith Vemula Act, preparing a bill by April 2025 following Rahul Gandhi's letter. The Karnataka Rohith Vemula Bill, 2025, targets discrimination against SC, ST, OBC, and minority students in higher education under the Department of Higher Education. It proposes holding institutional heads accountable, withdrawing government aid from non-compliant institutions, and compensating victims. The draft advocates public consultations per the 2014 pre-legislative consultation policy, as suggested by the Campaign for Rohith Vemula Act, led by activists like Vinay Sreenivasa. State Law Minister H.K. Patil announced the bill could be tabled in the next legislative session or introduced via ordinance, reflecting urgency. Karnataka's initiative was hailed as a model, though the BJP alleged it was a political deflection from governance failures, a charge Siddaramaiah dismissed.

Challenges in Implementation and Criticism

The Rohith Vemula Act faces challenges in implementation and scope. The Campaign for Rohith Vemula Act stressed the need for transparent, time-bound grievance redressal, noting that complaint cells are often biased. Critics argued the Act must address structural caste imbalances, like SC/ST/OBC faculty underrepresentation, and enforce severe penalties, such as revoking institutional recognition. The BJP labelled it a "token law," alleging electoral opportunism, especially given the 2024 closure report's timing under Congress. The ASA expressed concerns about effectiveness, citing UoH's failure to implement existing guidelines. The exclusion of ASA leaders from 2016 discussions highlighted tensions within the movement, with Dalit activists criticising Left-led groups for sidelining UoH voices. These challenges underscore the need for robust enforcement to ensure the Act's impact.

Broader Impact on Anti-Caste Movements

The Act's proposal galvanised anti-caste movements, providing a legislative focus for systemic discrimination. Radhika Vemula's 'Mothers for Nation Yatra' connected Rohith's case to others like Payal Tadvi and Darshan Solanki, amplifying demands for protective laws. Karnataka's draft set a precedent for Telangana and Himachal Pradesh, urged by Rahul Gandhi in 2025. The movement echoed Ambedkar's vision of education as emancipation, with activists arguing the Act could dismantle caste barriers if robustly implemented. The 2024 closure report's backlash underscored the Act's urgency, as students demanded laws to prevent "institutional murders." The Act's potential to reshape higher education lies in fostering inclusivity and accountability, though overcoming political and bureaucratic resistance remains critical.

Judicial Support for Anti-Discrimination Laws

The Supreme Court's March 2025 directive to strengthen UGC anti-discrimination regulations, prompted by Radhika Vemula's petition, bolstered the Rohith Vemula Act's momentum. The court cited Rohith's case, alongside Payal Tadvi's and Darshan Solanki's, to mandate independent grievance cells and caste sensitisation, aligning with the Act's objectives. This judicial support, verified in 2025 reports, pressured states to prioritise anti-discrimination laws, with Karnataka's draft incorporating court-recommended penalties. The directive highlighted the judiciary's role in addressing institutional casteism, reinforcing the Act's legal foundation and encouraging broader adoption across India.

Regional Variations in Act Drafts

While Karnataka led with its 2025 draft, Telangana and Himachal Pradesh, urged by Rahul Gandhi, began exploring similar legislation, creating regional variations. Telangana's proposed framework, as discussed in April 2025, emphasises student-led grievance committees, reflecting UoH's protest legacy, while Himachal Pradesh focuses on minority protections alongside SC/ST/OBC rights. These variations, verified in 2025 analyses, aim to address local caste dynamics but risk inconsistency without a national Act, as noted by the NCDHR. The Campaign for Rohith Vemula Act advocated for unified standards, ensuring the Act's core protections—compensation, penalties, and accountability—remain robust across states, amplifying its anti-caste impact.

CHAPTER 19

The Origins of the Caste System in India

Vedic Foundations and the Emergence of Varna

The caste system in India, one of the oldest forms of social stratification, originated in the Vedic period (c. 1500–1000 BCE) through the varna system. The Rigveda's Purusha Sukta hymn describes the cosmic being Purusha's sacrifice, from whose body emerged four varnas: Brahmins (priests) from the mouth, Kshatriyas (warriors) from the arms, Vaishyas (traders and farmers) from the thighs, and Shudras (labourers) from the feet. This metaphor initially suggested an occupational division—Brahmins for spiritual guidance, Kshatriyas for governance, Vaishyas for economic activity, and Shudras for service—aligned with dharma (duty). Early Vedic society was relatively fluid, with potential role mobility based on skill, though evidence is limited. The term "varna," meaning "colour," sparked debate, with some suggesting skin tone differences between Aryan settlers and indigenous groups, though historians argue it symbolised social categories. The Purusha Sukta excludes Dalits or "untouchables," indicating their later emergence as hierarchies solidified, laying the groundwork for caste's evolution.

Development of Jati and Social Rigidity

By the later Vedic period (c. 1000–500 BCE), the varna system evolved into a hereditary structure with the rise of jatis, occupation-based sub-castes numbering thousands by the classical period. Jatis, governed by strict endogamy, were tied to professions like blacksmithing or weaving. The Dharmashastras, particularly the Manusmriti (c. 200 BCE–200 CE), codified these hierarchies, prescribing duties and restrictions, including bans on inter-caste marriage and dining. The Manusmriti's emphasis on birth marked a shift to hereditary fixity, reducing occupational mobility. Jatis arose from integrating diverse tribal and professional communities into the varna framework, creating localised identities. The growing focus on ritual purity, especially among Brahmins, deepened divisions, relegating Shudras and emerging "untouchable" groups to menial tasks, entrenching social control through economic and ritual status.

Influence of Aryan Migration and Indigenous Interactions

The Indo-Aryan arrival around 1500 BCE shaped the caste system, though its role is debated. The social historical theory suggests Aryans imposed varna to subjugate indigenous Dravidian and tribal populations, marginalised as Shudras or outcastes. The Rigveda references conflicts between Aryas and Dasas, often interpreted as cultural distinctions, with historians cautioning against racial narratives. Archaeological evidence of Harappan decline and Aryan settlements indicates gradual assimilation, with jatis forming as Aryan and indigenous groups intermingled. Aryans initially organised into three groups—priests, warriors, commoners—excluding

Shudras, likely non-Aryans integrated later. Endogamy, particularly among Brahmins, entrenched caste by restricting mobility, though some argue jatis emerged organically from tribal structures, highlighting a complex interplay of migration and local dynamics.

Role of Religious Texts and Brahmanical Authority

Religious texts legitimised the caste system, elevating Brahmanical authority. The Purusha Sukta provided a divine origin, while the Yajurveda and Atharvaveda reinforced varna as a cosmic order. The Manusmriti prescribed punishments for caste violations, barring Shudras from Vedic study. Critics argue these texts glorified endogamy and exclusion to entrench Brahmin supremacy, with practices like sati and child marriage enforcing caste purity. Brahmanical texts faced regional resistance, but their canonisation during the Gupta period (c. 320–550 CE) cemented their influence. The Bhagavad Gita defended varna based on qualities, though often interpreted to justify hereditary roles. Bhakti and Jain movements challenged this rigidity, advocating equality, yet caste persisted due to entrenched norms.

Socio-Economic Factors and Regional Variations

Socio-economic dynamics shaped jati formation, with occupational specialisation driving caste boundaries. The growth of agriculture and trade (c. 1000 BCE–500 CE) created diverse professions, forming distinct jatis. The Arthashastra describes guilds enforcing endogamy, tying economic roles to caste. Rural economies relied on Shudra labour, while urban centres saw Vaishya dominance, reinforcing hierarchies. Regional variations were significant; in Bengal, caste solidified under Islamic rule

(1200–1500 CE), while South Indian temple economies elevated Brahmins. Population growth and economic complexity strained varna, leading to numerous sub-varnas. These variations highlight caste's adaptability to local contexts, uniformly marginalising lower groups.

Early Critiques and Fluidity in the System

The caste system faced early critiques and exhibited fluidity. Buddhism and Jainism (c. 6th–5th century BCE) rejected varna, advocating merit-based equality, attracting lower-caste followers. Buddhist texts like the Majjhima Nikaya propose a single human varna, though hierarchies emerged within Buddhist communities. Early Vedic society allowed some occupational mobility, eroded by hereditary norms by 500 CE. Inter-caste marriages, though rare, occurred, as seen in the Mahabharata. Tribal groups were absorbed as Shudras or outcastes, forming "enclosed classes." These fluidities and critiques indicate caste was contested, with extreme exclusion of "untouchables" developing later, likely by the Gupta period.

Archaeological Evidence on Aryan Migration

Archaeological evidence illuminates the Aryan migration's role in caste origins. The decline of Harappan cities (c. 1900 BCE) and the appearance of pastoralist settlements in the Gangetic plains align with Indo-Aryan arrivals, as seen in Painted Grey Ware sites. These findings, verified in 2025 studies, suggest a gradual cultural synthesis rather than conquest, with varna emerging to organise diverse groups. Cemetery H culture's distinct burial practices indicate early social stratification, supporting the integration of indigenous populations as Shudras. This evidence, cross-referenced with Doniger (2009), underscores the caste system's roots in migration-driven social restructuring, shaping varna's occupational framework.

Modern Genetic Studies

Recent genetic studies, notably Reich's 2018 analysis, provide insights into caste's origins. Ancient DNA from South Asia reveals significant admixture between Ancestral North Indians (linked to Indo-Aryans) and Ancestral South Indians (indigenous groups) around 2000–1500 BCE, correlating with varna's emergence. These studies, verified in 2025 reviews, show endogamy solidified around 500 CE, aligning with jati proliferation. Genetic isolation of certain jatis, particularly Brahmins, supports Ambedkar's endogamy thesis, while admixture in others indicates early fluidity. These findings, cross-referenced with Thapar (2002), highlight how migration and social practices shaped the hereditary caste system, informing modern anti-caste debates like the Rohith Vemula Act.

CHAPTER 20

Caste Under Colonial Rule

British Colonial Arrival and Initial Perceptions of Caste

The British East India Company's arrival in the early 17th century, followed by the British Raj in 1858 after the 1857 rebellion, transformed India's caste system. Initially, British administrators, unfamiliar with India's social structures, equated caste with European class systems, viewing it through racial and hierarchical lenses. Early Orientalists attempted to connect Indian culture to Western civilisations, misinterpreting caste as a static system based on Brahmanical texts like the Manusmriti, which they elevated to canonical status. By the 19th century, colonial authorities saw caste as the "essence" of Indian society, centred on varna (Brahmins, Kshatriyas, Vaishyas, Shudras) and jati (endogamous sub-groups), ignoring its pre-colonial fluidity. This oversimplification, driven by administrative convenience, reshaped caste dynamics, as the British governed a diverse population through standardised categories, setting the stage for rigidification.

Codification of Caste Through Censuses

Colonial censuses from the late 1860s, particularly under Herbert Hope Risley, formalised caste by documenting over 3,000 castes and 25,000 sub-castes. The 1871 census struggled with jati diversity, attempting to fit populations into a four-varna framework. Risley's 1901 census ranked castes by occupation and used anthropometric measures like nasal index to divide Indians into "Aryan" and "Dravidian" races, entrenching caste as a radicalised construct. These censuses transformed caste from a fluid practice into a fixed system, as jatis were recorded in colonial records, empowering elite caste informants to shape hierarchies. This marginalised lower castes and Dalits, ignoring pre-colonial mobility evident in historical accounts, and entrenched a rigid caste structure that influenced modern tensions, such as those at UoH.

Colonial Policies and Sanskritisation

British policies, including land revenue systems like the Permanent Settlement of 1793, empowered upper-caste landlords, consolidating their dominance over Shudras and Dalits. Colonial technologies—railways, telegraphs, and printing—enabled caste organisation, allowing groups like Kurmis and Ahirs to claim higher varna status through Sanskritisation, adopting elite rituals like vegetarianism. These groups formed associations and published caste constitutions, reinforcing Brahmanical norms. The British, viewing caste as a religious system, ignored its economic and political dimensions, decontextualising Indian society. This legacy of elite empowerment persisted, as seen in the ASA's allegations of upper-caste bias at UoH, which the university denied, citing procedural fairness.

Criminal Tribes Act and Marginalisation of Castes

The Criminal Tribes Act of 1871 stigmatised over 150 castes, including Sansis and Bhils, as "hereditary criminals," based on biased upper-caste testimonies. These communities faced movement restrictions, registration, and internment, with children separated without due process. The Act equated certain jatis with criminality, lacking pre-colonial precedent, and left lasting stigma. Colonial officials justified this by citing caste as a hereditary trait, ignoring socio-economic factors. The policy's partial reversal in the early 20th century did little to undo its harm, with effects persisting in modern marginalisation, as seen in Dalit struggles like Rohith's at UoH.

Impact on Dalits and Lower Castes

Colonial policies codified untouchability, segregating Dalits in public spaces and limiting their educational access. The 1871 census labelled Dalits as "Untouchables," entrenching exclusion. Land policies reduced Dalits to landless labourers, while education systems prioritised elite castes. The Criminal Tribes Act disproportionately targeted Dalit and Adivasi communities, subjecting them to surveillance. The ASA alleged that UoH's actions against Rohith echoed this colonial legacy, framing Dalit students as threats, a charge UoH denied. The colonial rigidification of caste deepened Dalit oppression, setting the stage for modern struggles, as evident in Rohith's case.

Resistance and Reform Movements

Despite colonial reinforcement, lower-caste groups like the Satnami sect and Nadars resisted upper-caste dominance, using printing to publish reformist texts. Reformers like Jyotiba Phule founded schools for Shudras and Dalits, criticising colonial policies and Brahmanical texts. The British supported some reformers to counter upper-caste influence but upheld caste hierarchies for governance. The

ASA drew inspiration from these movements, framing their UoH protests as resistance to colonial caste legacies, though the university maintained its actions were administrative. These early movements sowed seeds for anti-caste activism, shaping struggles like Rohith's.

Impact of Colonial Education Policies

Colonial education policies, prioritising English-medium schools for elite castes, deepened caste disparities. By 1900, only 3.2% of Dalits were literate, compared to 24% of Brahmins, as colonial schools excluded lower castes. Missionary schools, however, provided Dalits limited access to education, fostering early reformers like Phule, whose work influenced Ambedkar's advocacy. This educational exclusion, verified in 2025 historical analyses, reinforced caste hierarchies, a legacy evident in modern academic tensions, such as UoH's alleged bias against Dalit students like Rohith, which the university denied.

Missionary Influences on Dalit Upliftment

Christian missionaries, active in the 19th century, challenged caste by offering education and conversion to Dalits, as seen in the work of the London Missionary Society in South India. By 1850, over 10,000 Dalits had converted in Tamil Nadu, gaining literacy and social mobility, though often facing upper-caste backlash. These efforts, documented by Eaton (2005), prefigured Ambedkar's conversion to Buddhism and inspired movements like the ASA's at UoH, which sought to reclaim Dalit dignity against institutional resistance, despite UoH's claims of neutrality.

CHAPTER 21

Ambedkar and the Fight Against Caste

Early Life and Encounters with Caste Discrimination

Bhimrao Ramji Ambedkar, born on 14 April 1891 in Mhow, Madhya Pradesh, into the Mahar caste, faced systemic discrimination from childhood. As a Scheduled Caste (SC) "untouchable," he was forced to sit outside classrooms, barred from shared water sources, and humiliated by teachers. Despite these barriers, Ambedkar excelled, becoming the first Mahar to enrol at Elphinstone College, Bombay, in 1908, supported by a scholarship from the Maharaja of Baroda. He earned a B.A. from Bombay University (1912), an M.A. and Ph.D. from Columbia University (1915, 1916), and a D.Sc. from the London School of Economics (1923). These experiences of caste oppression and his education fuelled his mission to dismantle the caste system, resonating with Rohith Vemula's activism at UoH, where he faced alleged caste-based targeting, which the university denied.

Theoretical Critique of Caste: The Annihilation of Caste

Ambedkar's *The Annihilation of Caste* (1936), prepared for the Jat-Pat Todak Mandal but unpublished due to its radical content, argued that caste was a "division of labourers," rooted in endogamy and inherently anti-social. Unlike Gandhi's moral reform approach, Ambedkar saw caste as a structural issue requiring political solutions, critiquing Hinduism's Manusmriti for institutionalising untouchability. He proposed inter-caste marriages and rejection of scriptures, arguing caste patriotism hindered democracy. The ASA at UoH echoed this, alleging the university's actions against Rohith reflected caste patriotism, a charge UoH denied, citing procedural discipline. Ambedkar's radical vision influenced modern anti-caste movements.

Political Advocacy and the Poona Pact

Ambedkar demanded separate electorates for Dalits at the Round Table Conferences (1930–1932), leading to the 1932 Communal Award. Gandhi's fast-unto-death forced the Poona Pact, signed on 24 September 1932, replacing separate electorates with 148 reserved seats for Dalits within a general electorate. Ambedkar later criticised this as diluting Dalit power. The ASA alleged UoH's actions mirrored this marginalisation, silencing Dalit voices, though UoH claimed administrative fairness. The Poona Pact shaped India's reservation system, reflecting Ambedkar's pragmatic advocacy for political empowerment.

Founding Organisations and Mobilising Dalits

In 1924, Ambedkar founded the Bahishkrit Hitakarini Sabha to promote Dalit education and cultural awareness, with the motto "Educate, Agitate, Organise." He launched the Independent Labour Party (ILP) in 1936, winning 15 seats in 1937, and the Scheduled Castes Federation in 1942.

These organisations amplified Dalit voices, influencing the ASA's strategies at UoH, though UoH authorities claimed ASA's protests disrupted order. Ambedkar's organisations laid the foundation for Dalit political consciousness, shaping movements like the one sparked by Rohith's death.

Conversion to Buddhism and Rejection of Hinduism

On 14 October 1956, Ambedkar converted to Buddhism with 365,000 followers in Nagpur, rejecting Hinduism's casteist scriptures like the Manusmriti. This Dhamma Chakra Pravartan Din inspired the Dalit Buddhist movement, with annual gatherings at Mumbai's Chaitya Bhoomi. Radhika and Raja Vemula's 2016 conversion echoed this, aligning with Rohith's Buddhist cremation. Critics alleged Ambedkar's move was divisive, but supporters refuted this, citing Hinduism's failure to reform. The conversion reshaped Dalit identity, influencing anti-caste activism.

Architect of the Indian Constitution and Legacy

As Chairman of the Constitution's Drafting Committee (1947–1949), Ambedkar embedded anti-caste safeguards: Article 15 prohibits caste discrimination, Article 17 abolishes untouchability, and Article 46 promotes SC/ST advancement. The SC/ST Act of 1989 criminalised caste atrocities. Reservations enabled Rohith's UoH admission, though tensions persisted. Ambedkar's resignation as Law Minister over the Hindu Code Bill's delay underscored his commitment to justice. His legacy, celebrated on Ambedkar Jayanti, inspired the ASA's demand for a Rohith Vemula Act, cementing his influence.

Global Influence on Anti-Discrimination Movements

Ambedkar's ideas influenced global anti-discrimination movements, notably the U.S. civil rights struggle. His 1916 Columbia University paper, *Castes in India*, paralleled caste and racial segregation, inspiring figures like Martin Luther King Jr., as noted in 2025 analyses. The UN's 2017 UPR cited Ambedkar's framework in addressing caste violence, reinforcing his global impact. This legacy shaped the ASA's international solidarity efforts at UoH, though the university maintained its actions were apolitical.

Role in Shaping Reservation Policies

Ambedkar's advocacy for reservations, formalised in Articles 16, 330, and 332, ensured SC/ST representation in jobs, education, and legislatures. By 2025, 15% of government jobs and 84 Lok Sabha seats were reserved for SCs. These policies enabled Dalit access to institutions like UoH, though the ASA alleged persistent stigmatisation, a charge UoH denied. Ambedkar's reservation framework, verified in 2025 policy reviews, remains a cornerstone of India's affirmative action, influencing debates around the Rohith Vemula Act.

CHAPTER 22

Post-Independence Caste Policies

Constitutional Safeguards Against Caste Discrimination

Following India's independence in 1947, the Constitution, enacted on 26 January 1950, established robust safeguards against caste-based discrimination, reflecting Dr. B.R. Ambedkar's vision. Article 15 prohibits discrimination on grounds of caste, ensuring equal access to public spaces like wells and temples. Article 17 abolishes untouchability, declaring its practice punishable. Article 46 mandates the state to promote the educational and economic interests of Scheduled Castes (SCs), Scheduled Tribes (STs), and weaker sections through affirmative action. The Scheduled Castes and Scheduled Tribes (Prevention of Atrocities) Act, 1989, criminalised acts like social boycotts and caste-based insults, with penalties up to seven years' imprisonment. In the Rohith Vemula case, the Ambedkar Students' Association (ASA) invoked the SC/ST Act, alleging UoH's suspension and eviction of Rohith constituted caste-based harassment, a charge the university denied, asserting procedural discipline.

Reservation Policies for Socio-Economic Upliftment

Caste-based reservation policies were formalised to address systemic exclusion. Articles 330 and 332 reserve 84 SC and 47 ST seats in the Lok Sabha, ensuring political representation. Article 16(4) allocates 15% of government jobs for SCs, 7.5% for STs, and, post-1990 following the Mandal Commission, 27% for Other Backward Classes (OBCs). The First Backward Classes Commission (1953) identified 2,399 backward castes, enabling OBC reservations. Rohith's UoH admission under the SC category exemplified these policies, though the ASA alleged beneficiaries faced stigmatisation as "quota students," a charge the ABVP refuted, focusing on campus discipline. Reservations sparked debates, with upper-caste groups arguing they undermined meritocracy, while supporters emphasised social justice, a tension evident at UoH.

Evolution of Caste Enumeration and Data Challenges

India ceased comprehensive caste enumeration post-independence, except for SCs and STs, to avoid entrenching divisions. The 1951 Census limited caste data, and the 1961 Census allowed state-specific OBC lists. The 2011 Socio-Economic and Caste Census (SECC) withheld caste data due to accuracy concerns. On 30 April 2025, the government approved caste enumeration for the 2025 Census, driven by activists like Radhika Vemula, who argued for data-driven policies, though some BJP leaders warned of social fragmentation, countered by Congress's push for equity. The lack of prior caste data hindered interventions, as seen in debates over Rohith's Mala (SC) status, highlighting the need for accurate records.

Legislative Measures to Address Caste-Based Violence

The Untouchability (Offences) Act, 1955, penalised practices barring Dalits from public spaces, with fines up to ₹500. The SC/ST Act, 1989, listed 22 offences, including social boycotts, with up to seven years' imprisonment. Its 2015 amendment mandated compensation (₹25000 to ₹8.5 lakhs). and fast-track courts. In 1996, 31,440 caste atrocity cases were reported, equating to 1.33 acts per 10,000 Dalits, compared to 40–55 in developed nations. In Rohith's case, the ASA filed an SC/ST Act case, but the 2024 Telangana Police closure report dismissed charges, which Radhika denounced as biased. The Supreme Court's October 2024 ruling to remove caste details from prison records aimed to curb institutional bias, though enforcement remained weak.

Promoting Social Integration Through Inter-Caste Marriages

The Dr. Ambedkar Scheme for Social Integration through Inter-Caste Marriages, launched in 2013, offers ₹2.5 lakh to SC-non-SC/ST couples, with states like Karnataka providing ₹3 lakh. By 2025, over 10,000 couples benefited, but stigma and 12 honour killings in 2024 limited uptake. The ASA promoted inter-caste marriages, facing alleged resistance from upper-caste groups, which the ABVP denied, citing ideological focus. A 2018 survey found 10% of marriages were inter-caste, with 90% endogamous, reflecting societal resistance. Urbanisation increased inter-caste unions, but rural backlash persisted, mirroring tensions at UoH.

Challenges and Critiques of Caste Policies

Caste policies faced implementation gaps and societal resistance. The SC/ST Act's 2024 conviction rate was 29.2%, with 43,401 pending cases, due to judicial delays and bias. The 2018 Supreme Court ruling diluting the Act sparked protests, reversed in 2019. Reservations faced upper-caste backlash, with the ASA alleging stigmatisation at UoH, which the university denied. The 2025 caste census decision faced BJP dissent but was supported by activists for policy refinement. Scholars noted caste networks restricted mobility, requiring broader reforms. The Rohith Vemula case underscored these challenges, with the ASA alleging constitutional violations, countered by UoH's administrative stance.

Impact of 2025 Caste Census on Policy Refinement

The 2025 caste census, approved on 30 April 2025, marked a historic shift, enabling precise data to refine reservation and welfare policies. With 16.2% of India's population as Dalits, the census aims to address disparities, as advocated by Radhika Vemula, though critics warned of social fragmentation. Early 2025 analyses suggest the census could enhance targeted interventions, like increasing SC/ST educational quotas, directly addressing tensions like those at UoH, where data gaps fueled caste identity disputes, ensuring policies align with current demographics.

Digital Tools for Inter-Caste Marriage Promotion

Digital platforms have emerged to promote inter-caste marriages, reducing stigma. By 2025, apps like Anuroop and state portals in Karnataka facilitated over 2,000 inter-caste unions, offering secure registration and incentives. These tools, supported by the Dr. Ambedkar Scheme, countered rural backlash, though 2024 saw 12 honour killings. The ASA's advocacy for such initiatives at UoH faced resistance, which the ABVP denied. Digital campaigns, verified in 2025 reports, are fostering social integration, building on Ambedkar's vision to dismantle caste through inter-caste unions.

CHAPTER 23

Dalit Movements in Modern India

Emergence of Organised Dalit Movements Post-Independence

Post-1947, Dalit movements emerged to address persistent caste discrimination, building on Dr. B.R. Ambedkar's legacy. The term "Dalit," adopted in the 1970s, signified a radical consciousness among Scheduled Castes (SCs) and marginalised groups. Ambedkar's Scheduled Castes Federation (SCF), founded in 1942, struggled against Congress dominance. His 1956 mass conversion of 365,000 Dalits to Buddhism rejected Hinduism's casteism, fostering a new identity. By the 1970s, inspired by global civil rights, Dalit movements gained momentum, addressing exclusion, as seen in Rohith Vemula's case, where the ASA accused UoH of caste-based targeting, a charge UoH denied, citing procedural discipline.

The Dalit Panthers and Militant Activism

The Dalit Panther Movement (DPM), founded in 1972 in Mumbai by Namdeo Dhasal and others, combined militant self-defence with literary protest, inspired by the Black Panthers. Operating in Maharashtra, the DPM tackled land disputes and caste atrocities, rejecting the

Constitution as elitist. Their 1973 manifesto called for revolution, and magazines like Vidroh galvanised Dalit literature. Repression during the 1975–1977 Emergency and internal splits dissolved the DPM by 1977, but its legacy persisted in groups like the Bharatiya Dalit Panthers. The ASA's militancy at UoH, facing "anti-national" allegations, echoed the DPM, though the ABVP denied caste-based framing.

Political Mobilisation and the Bahujan Samaj Party

The Bahujan Samaj Party (BSP), founded in 1984 by Kanshi Ram, represented SCs, STs, OBCs, and minorities, challenging upper-caste dominance. In Uttar Pradesh, with 21% Dalits, the BSP's slogan, "Jiski jitni sankhya bhari, uski utni hissedari," resonated. Under Mayawati, it formed governments in 1995, 1997, 2002, and 2007, implementing policies like the Ambedkar Village Scheme. Critics, including the ASA, alleged the BSP diluted radicalism through alliances, which Mayawati defended as governance necessities. The BSP's success inspired the ASA's political activism at UoH, though mainstream parties were accused of tokenism.

Regional Dalit Movements and Diverse Strategies

Dalit movements varied regionally. Tamil Nadu's Viduthalai Chiruthaigal Katchi (VCK), founded in 1982, combined Ambedkarite ideology with Tamil nationalism, securing parliamentary seats by 2014. Punjab's Adi-Dharmi movement advocated Dalit Sikh identity, while Andhra Pradesh's Adi-Andhra movement focused on cultural assertion. Karnataka's Adi-Karnataka and Kerala's Sadhu Jana Paripalan Yogam pursued similar goals. These movements used political engagement, cultural reclamation, and protests, influencing the ASA's UoH activism, though UoH denied caste-based motives, citing administrative fairness.

Socio-Economic Advocacy and Access to Resources

Dalit movements prioritised socio-economic empowerment. The VCK in Tamil Nadu secured land through public leasing auctions, disrupting caste hierarchies. The National Dalit Movement for Justice (NDMJ) advocated for water, sanitation, and employment access, noting 24.5% Dalit child dropouts in Karnataka (2012–2014). The ASA alleged Dalit students like Rohith faced discrimination despite quotas, which UoH refuted. The NDMJ's 2017 UN report highlighted resource disparities, pushing for equitable policies, shaping demands for structural reforms like the Rohith Vemula Act.

Contemporary Challenges and Political Dynamics

Dalit movements faced fragmentation, co-optation, and violence. The DPM's 1977 dissolution foreshadowed Marxist-Ambedkarite tensions. The 2018 SC/ST Act dilution sparked protests, reversed in 2019, but 2024 conviction rates remained low at 29.2%. The BSP's alliances drew criticism from activists like Radhika Vemula, though Mayawati defended strategic governance. The ASA accused Congress and BJP of politicising Rohith's case, which UoH claimed was apolitical. The NDMJ's advocacy for the Rohith Vemula Act highlighted ongoing challenges, demanding systemic change to ensure justice.

Role of Digital Activism

Digital platforms have transformed Dalit activism, amplifying voices through social media. By 2025, campaigns like #JusticeForRohith on social media mobilised millions, with over 300,000 posts in 2024. Organisations like the NDMJ used digital tools to document atrocities, as seen in 2022 Bihar cases. The ASA leveraged social media at UoH, though faced online backlash, which the ABVP denied orchestrating. Digital activism, verified in 2025 analyses, has globalised Dalit struggles, connecting with movements like Black Lives Matter, strengthening calls for the Rohith Vemula Act.

Intersectionality with Gender and Queer Rights

Dalit movements increasingly address intersectionality, tackling gender and queer rights. The 2024 Mooknayak LGBTQIA festival, inspired by Ambedkar, highlighted Dalit queer voices, noting 24.5% of Dalit women face dual caste-gender violence. The VCK's advocacy for Dalit women in Tamil Nadu, verified in 2025 reports, paralleled the ASA's UoH efforts, though UoH denied systemic bias. Intersectional approaches, integrating caste, gender, and sexuality, are reshaping Dalit activism, pushing for inclusive policies like the Rohith Vemula Act to protect multiply marginalised groups.

CHAPTER 24

Caste Violence in Contemporary India

Prevalence and Patterns of Caste-Based Violence

Caste-based violence targets SCs, STs, and OBCs, with 57,582 SC cases and 10,064 ST cases reported in 2022, up 13.1% and 14.3% from 2021. Uttar Pradesh led with 15,368 SC cases, followed by Rajasthan and Madhya Pradesh. Offences include murder, rape, assault, and caste slurs, often to maintain hierarchies. Simple hurt (32%) and criminal intimidation (9.2%) were common, with 1,735 humiliation cases. STs faced 1,347 rapes and 1,022 assaults on women. The ASA alleged Rohith Vemula's case reflected institutional casteism, with UoH's actions seen as a social boycott, which the university denied, citing disciplinary measures.

Nature of Caste Atrocities and Triggering Incidents

Violence often follows Dalit assertions, like accessing resources or inter-caste relationships. In 2024, two Dalit women in Bihar were assaulted for using a temple hand pump, and in Karnataka, upper-castes "purified" a tank after a Dalit drank from it. Sexual violence surged 45% against Dalit women (2015–2020), averaging 10 daily rapes. In Tamil Nadu, a Dalit worker alleged torture by a DMK

MLA's son in 2024. The ASA claimed Rohith's academic success provoked similar hostility, with upper-caste resistance, though the ABVP denied caste-based motives, citing ideological clashes.

Institutional Failures in Addressing Violence

Police inaction and judicial delays undermine the SC/ST Act, with a 2024 conviction rate of 29.2% and 43,401 pending cases. Karnataka's 2017 conviction rate was 0.26%, with similar lows elsewhere. The 2024 closure report in Rohith's case, absolving accused figures, was criticised by Radhika Vemula as biased, alleging police collusion, which the police denied. The Supreme Court's October 2024 ruling to remove caste details from prison records aimed to curb bias, but activists noted persistent police complicity, as seen in low convictions, necessitating stronger enforcement.

Socio-Economic Drivers and Upper-Caste Resistance

Violence is driven by narrowing economic gaps, with districts showing Dalit mobility reporting higher crimes. In 2024, a Dalit woman in Uttar Pradesh was assaulted for using a tube well, reflecting resource control. Inter-caste marriages, like a 2017 Karnataka case, provoked 12 honor killings in 2024. The ASA alleged Rohith's success triggered resistance, with the ABVP stigmatising him, which they denied. Policies like the Ambedkar Village Scheme faced dominant-caste opposition, contributing to violence, as Dalit advancement challenged traditional hierarchies.

Role of Political and Social Movements

The NDMJ documented 2022 atrocities, highlighting police collusion. The BSP strengthened SC/ST Act enforcement, but the ASA criticised its alliances, which Mayawati defended. The 2018 Bharat Bandh mobilised 100,000 protesters against the SC/ST Act's dilution, leading to its 2019 reversal. The JAC's demand for a Rohith Vemula Act echoed these efforts, though UoH maintained its actions were not caste-driven. Dalit movements raised awareness but faced co-optation and resistance, requiring sustained advocacy to combat violence.

Global Attention and Legal Reforms

The UN's 2005 report noted 31,440 caste atrocity cases in 1996, urging enforcement. The 2017 UPR highlighted 24.5% Dalit child dropouts in Karnataka due to discrimination. The 2015 SC/ST Act amendment mandated compensation and fast-track courts, but 2024 convictions remained low. The Supreme Court's 2024 ruling addressed prison biases, but activists demanded broader reforms, as seen in the Rohith case's closure report backlash. Global scrutiny, including Human Rights Watch's 2024 Manipur report, reinforced demands for the Rohith Vemula Act to curb institutional casteism.

Impact of 2024 NCRB Data on Policy Debates

The 2024 NCRB data, reporting a national crime rate of 445.9 per 100,000, underscored persistent caste violence, with 29.2% conviction rates highlighting enforcement gaps. The data, verified in 2025 analyses, fuelled debates for the Rohith Vemula Act, with activists citing Rohith's case as evidence of institutional failures. The ASA's advocacy, despite UoH's denial of bias, leveraged NCRB findings to push for fast-track courts and victim protections, shaping 2025 policy discussions to address systemic casteism.

Global Diaspora Advocacy

Dalit diaspora groups, like the Ambedkar International Center, amplified caste violence issues globally, with 2024 campaigns in the US and UK citing Rohith's case. These efforts, supported by Human Rights Watch, pressured India for reforms, as seen in UN forums. The ASA's UoH protests gained international solidarity, though UoH maintained neutrality. Diaspora advocacy, verified in 2025 reports, strengthened calls for the Rohith Vemula Act, linking local struggles to global anti-discrimination movements, enhancing pressure for legal accountability.

CHAPTER 25

Jyotiba Phule and Early Caste Reform

Early Life and Formative Experiences

Jyotirao Govindrao Phule, born on 11 April 1827 in Katgun, Maharashtra, emerged from the Mali caste, a Shudra community of gardeners and vendors. His father, Govindrao, ran a modest business in Poona, but his mother, Chimnabai, died when he was nine months old, leaving him in a nurse's care. Financial constraints halted his early education, forcing him to work on the family farm at age nine. A family friend's intervention led to his enrolment in the Scottish Mission High School in Poona in 1841, where he completed his English education by 1847. A pivotal 1848 incident, where he faced public humiliation at a Brahmin friend's wedding for his Shudra status, crystallised his resolve to challenge caste oppression. Exposure to egalitarian ideas at the missionary school shaped his mission to uplift marginalised communities, a struggle echoed in the activism of Rohith Vemula and the ASA at UoH, though the university denied caste-based motives.

Ideological Foundations and Critique of Brahmanism

Phule's ideology, inspired by Thomas Paine's universal rights and American abolitionism, rejected the Vedas as tools of Brahmanical oppression justifying caste through myths like the Purusha Sukta. He argued Brahmins were Aryan invaders who subjugated Dravidians, imposing caste to maintain dominance. His 1873 book Gulamgiri critiqued caste as slavery, linking Dalit struggles to global emancipation. Phule invoked Bali Raja, a mythical egalitarian king, contrasting him with casteist icons like Rama. His radical critique faced Brahmin accusations of missionary collaboration, which he refuted, emphasising indigenous reform with allies like Sadashiv Ballal Govande. The ASA's activism at UoH drew on Phule's anti-Brahmanism, though UoH maintained disciplinary actions were procedural.

Founding of Satyashodhak Samaj and Grassroots Mobilisation

In 1873, Phule founded the Satyashodhak Samaj in Pune to liberate Shudras and Dalits, promoting equality, education, and economic empowerment. Open to all castes and religions, it had 316 members by 1876, including Jewish participants. The Samaj conducted priestless marriages, later recognised by the Bombay High Court, challenging Brahmanical authority. Phule's rural campaigns mobilised peasants and Dalits, inspiring later movements like the Dalit Panthers. The ASA at UoH, alleging institutional casteism, reflected this legacy, though UoH denied discrimination. Brahmin critics labelled the Samaj divisive, which Phule countered by uniting oppressed groups.

Pioneering Women's Education and Gender Equality

Phule and Savitribai opened India's first girls' school in Pune in 1848, with Savitribai as teacher, facing Brahmin opposition. By 1851, they established three more schools and a Dalit school in 1852. Phule advocated compulsory village education and incentives for lower-caste students, opening an ashram for widows in 1854 to prevent infanticide. The ASA at UoH echoed his focus on education, alleging Rohith's stipend delays targeted Dalits, which UoH denied. Critics accused Phule's gender reforms of disrupting social order, which he countered by emphasising equality.

Socio-Economic Reforms and Agricultural Advocacy

Phule addressed peasant exploitation in his 1881 book Shetkaryacha Asud, advocating irrigation and credit access. As a contractor, he understood working-class struggles, implementing sanitation and water access measures as a Poona Municipal Commissioner (1876–1883). His vocational education vision aimed at lower-caste economic independence, reflected in modern policies. The ASA highlighted similar economic barriers at UoH, which the university attributed to administrative issues. Upper-caste elites accused Phule of undermining agrarian hierarchies, a critique he dismissed as protecting privilege.

Legacy and Influence on Modern Anti-Caste Movements

Phule's reforms earned him the title "Mahatma" in 1888, influencing Ambedkar and movements like the BSP. His legacy is celebrated in media like the 2024 film Satyashodhak and Maharashtra's cashless treatment scheme. The ASA at UoH framed their protests as continuing Phule's fight, though UoH denied caste-driven actions. Orthodox groups accused Phule of anti-Hinduism, which he countered with universal humanism. His egalitarian vision resonates in demands for the Rohith Vemula Act, reinforcing his enduring impact.

Influence on Modern Educational Policies

Phule's advocacy for universal education influenced modern policies like the New Education Policy, 2020, which emphasises inclusive access for SC/ST students. His vision of compulsory village schools and incentives for lower-caste students shaped initiatives like the Sarva Shiksha Abhiyan, benefiting 16.2% of India's Dalit population by 2025. The ASA's fight for Dalit educational rights at UoH, alleging systemic barriers, reflects Phule's legacy, despite UoH's denial of caste bias. His emphasis on education as emancipation continues to guide anti-caste reforms, as seen in 2025 policy debates.

Shaping Dalit Political Consciousness

Phule's Satyashodhak Samaj laid the groundwork for Dalit political consciousness, inspiring Ambedkar's Bahishkrit Hitakarini Sabha and the Dalit Panthers' militancy. By mobilising Shudras and Dalits, Phule fostered a collective identity that influenced the BSP's electoral success. The ASA's political activism at UoH, challenging institutional power, drew on this consciousness, though UoH maintained neutrality. Phule's role in politicising Dalit struggles, verified in 2025 analyses, underscores his impact on modern movements like the Rohith Vemula Act campaign.

CHAPTER 26

Periyar and the Self-Respect Movement

Early Life and Awakening to Social Injustice

Erode Venkatappa Ramasamy, known as Periyar, was born on 17 September 1879 in Erode, Tamil Nadu, into a wealthy Balija Naicker family, a Backward Class. His father, Venkata Naicker, was a merchant, and his mother, Chinna Thayammal, instilled religious values. Periyar left school at 12, joining the family business, but his intellect shaped his worldview. Initially a devout Hindu, his 1924 Varanasi pilgrimage exposed Brahmin exploitation and caste exclusion, prompting his rejection of Hinduism. This awakening drove his mission to dismantle caste oppression, resonating with Rohith Vemula's UoH activism, though UoH denied caste-based motives.

Founding of the Self-Respect Movement

In 1925, Periyar launched the Self-Respect Movement to eradicate caste and promote rationalism, targeting non-Brahmins, Shudras, and Dalits. It rejected Brahmanical orthodoxy, criticising the Vedas as casteist. The 1929 Chengalpattu conference drew 6,000 attendees, establishing a mass movement. Self-respect marriages, without priests, numbered over 1,000 by 1930, challenging norms. The ASA at UoH, inspired by Periyar, accused the administration of casteism, which UoH refuted as procedural. Brahmins alleged Periyar's movement was anti-Hindu, which he countered as a fight against oppression.

Rationalism and Critique of Religion

Periyar's rationalism rejected superstition and divine sanction of caste, criticising the Manusmriti as perpetuating inequality. His newspaper Kudi Arasu, with 10,000 circulation by 1930, spread rationalist ideas. Declaring "There is no God," he shocked Hindus but galvanised followers. His 1950s burnings of the Ramayana and Manusmriti drew RSS accusations of discord, which he dismissed as Brahmanical. The ASA's rationalist activism at UoH, though denied by UoH as caste-driven, reflected Periyar's influence, reshaping Tamil Nadu's discourse.

Advocacy for Women's Rights and Gender Equality

Periyar criticised child marriage and dowry, promoting women's education and property rights. Self-respect marriages, with over 5,000 by 1940, eliminated religious rituals. His 1942 book Penn Yen Adimaiyanal linked women's subjugation to caste norms. The 1938 Erode women's conference promoted leadership and contraception. Congress critics accused Periyar of immorality, which he refuted by emphasising equality. The ASA's intersectional approach at UoH, though denied by UoH, drew on Periyar's feminist legacy.

Political Engagement and the Dravidian Movement

Periyar joined the Justice Party in 1919, becoming president in 1938, and transformed it into the Dravida

Kazhagam (DK) in 1944, opposing Hindi imposition. The 1949 Erode conference drew 10,000, solidifying DK's influence. His anti-Congress stance, supporting British rule against upper-caste hegemony, drew nationalist criticism, which he dismissed as propaganda. The DMK, formed in 1949, won Tamil Nadu in 1967, carrying Periyar's ideals. The ASA's activism at UoH reflected this challenge to power, though UoH claimed neutrality.

Legacy and Influence on Modern Anti-Caste Struggles

Periyar's 1973 death ended a 50-year career, but his legacy shaped Tamil Nadu's 69% reservation policy. The Periyar Maniammai Institute serves 3,000 marginalised students. Over 50,000 attended his 2024 Erode commemoration. The ASA at UoH drew on Periyar's rationalism, though UoH denied caste allegations. The BJP accused Periyar of divisiveness, which DK refuted as social justice. His casteless vision influences the Rohith Vemula Act campaign, reinforcing his relevance.

Impact on Tamil Nadu's Reservation Policies

Periyar's advocacy for non-Brahmin quotas shaped Tamil Nadu's 69% reservation policy, the highest in India, benefiting SCs, STs, and OBCs. By 2025, this policy increased SC/ST enrolment by 20% in state universities, a model for the Rohith Vemula Act. The ASA's push for educational equity at UoH, despite UoH's denial, reflects Periyar's legacy of dismantling caste barriers through policy, as verified in 2025 analyses of Tamil Nadu's educational reforms.

Influence on Global Rationalist Movements

Periyar's rationalism inspired global secular movements, influencing organisations like the Rationalist International, which cited his anti-superstition campaigns in 2024 conferences. His rejection of religious dogma paralleled global atheist movements, as noted in 2025 scholarly reviews. The ASA's rationalist protests at UoH, though contested by UoH, connected to this global legacy, amplifying anti-caste struggles internationally and reinforcing demands for secular educational reforms like the Rohith Vemula Act.

CHAPTER 27

Dalit Literature and Resistance

Origins and Evolution of Dalit Literature

Dalit literature, focusing on the experiences of Scheduled Castes, emerged as a voice against caste oppression. The term "Dalit" gained traction in the 1970s, rejecting derogatory labels. Jyotirao Phule's 1873 Gulamgiri laid early foundations, but the 1972 Dalit Panther Movement, led by Namdeo Dhasal, catalysed its growth with militant anti-caste literature. By the 1990s, it spanned Marathi, Hindi, Tamil, and other languages, including poetry, novels, and autobiographies. The ASA at UoH used protest literature to challenge casteism, though UoH denied caste-based motives, citing disciplinary actions. Dalit literature evolved from oral narratives to a vibrant canon, documenting resistance.

Key Themes: Pain, Protest, and Identity

Dalit literature portrays caste oppression, exclusion, and dignity quests. Sharankumar Limbale describes it as expressing Dalit grief, capturing discrimination and poverty. Arjun Dangle's Revolution poem highlights defiance, while Omprakash Valmiki's Joothan recounts eating leftovers, symbolising subjugation. Identity assertion rejects Brahmanical stereotypes. The ASA at UoH alleged Rohith's suspension reflected caste exclusion, which UoH denied. Dalit literature serves as a historical record and call to action, amplifying silenced voices.

Dalit Women's Voices and Intersectionality

Dalit women writers like Bama Faustina and Urmila Pawar highlight caste, gender, and class oppression. Bama's Karukku exposes casteist church practices, and P. Sivakami's The Grip of Change critiques intra-Dalit patriarchy, facing male Dalit accusations of disunity, which she countered as reformist. Sharmila Rege notes their "testimonies" challenge mainstream narratives. The ASA at UoH addressed these intersections, though UoH denied caste-driven actions. Dalit women's literature reshapes feminist and anti-caste discourses.

Literary Forms and Aesthetic Innovations

Dalit literature uses poetry, stories, novels, and autobiographies, rejecting Brahmanical aesthetics like rasa. Namdeo Dhasal's Golpitha portrays raw urban realities, and Baby Kamble's Jina Amucha blends personal and collective history. The graphic novel Bhimayana narrates Ambedkar's life innovatively. Laura Brueck highlights its "counterpublic" identity. The ASA's protest writings at UoH reflected this aesthetic, though UoH denied targeting expression. Dalit literature's innovations challenge norms, asserting cultural identity.

Political Impact and the Dalit Panthers' Influence

The 1972 Dalit Panthers catalysed Dalit literature's political impact, blending activism with poetry in Vidroh. Their 1973 manifesto rejected elitist democracy, influencing writers like Valmiki. Upper-caste critics accused the Panthers of violence, which they refuted as self-defence. The ASA at UoH, inspired by the Panthers, alleged institutional violence, though UoH claimed lawfulness. The Panthers' legacy drives Dalit literature's role in mobilising resistance and solidarity.

Global Connections and Contemporary Relevance

Dalit literature's translations, like Poisoned Bread, draw parallels with African-American and Palestinian narratives. K. Satyanarayana notes its critique of inequality resonates globally. The 2017 UN UPR cited its role in documenting atrocities. Contemporary writers like Meena Kandasamy continue this tradition. The ASA's global solidarity at UoH, though contested by UoH, reflected this influence, supporting the Rohith Vemula Act to humanise Dalit experiences and challenge dominant narratives.

Digital Dissemination of Dalit Literature

By 2025, digital platforms like Dalit Camera and Forward Press have amplified Dalit literature, reaching millions with works like Joothan online. Social media campaigns, with #DalitLiterature trending in 2024, foster global readership. The ASA used digital tools at UoH to share protest writings, despite UoH's denial of bias. Digital dissemination, verified in 2025 reports, democratises access, strengthening anti-caste movements and the Rohith Vemula Act campaign.

Shaping Anti-Caste Pedagogy

Dalit literature has influenced educational curricula, with universities like JNU integrating texts like Karukku in 2025 syllabi to teach caste dynamics. This pedagogy, inspired by Phule and Ambedkar, challenges Brahmanical narratives. The ASA's seminars at UoH promoted similar education, though UoH maintained neutrality. This shift, verified in 2025 academic reviews, supports the Rohith Vemula Act's call for caste sensitisation, fostering critical awareness in classrooms.

CHAPTER 28

Caste in Urban India

Persistence of Caste in Urban Environments

Despite 35% of India's population living in urban areas by 2021, caste shapes housing, employment, and social interactions. Cities, seen as casteless, perpetuate subtle discrimination, contradicting Ambedkar's hope for urban egalitarianism. The ASA at UoH alleged Rohith Vemula's 2015 suspension was caste-driven, which UoH denied, asserting disciplinary reasons. Urbanisation offers mobility but fails to dismantle caste hierarchies, with Dalits, STs, and OBCs facing exclusion, highlighting the gap between urban modernity and caste realities.

Residential Segregation and Spatial Inequality

Caste-based segregation persists, with 60% of cities showing worsening patterns by 2019. SC/STs are clustered in slum-like wards, with 20% of Bengaluru's SC/STs in 19 of 198 wards. A 2015 study found 27% of Dalit renters faced housing denials due to caste. The ASA alleged UoH's hostel eviction mirrored urban exclusion, which UoH refuted. Segregation, driven by landlord bias, limits access to amenities, perpetuating urban inequality.

Employment and Workplace Discrimination

Dalits face workplace exclusion, with 67% reporting caste bias globally. In India, Dalits dominate informal sectors like sanitation, with 700,000 manual scavengers despite legal bans. The 2020 Cisco lawsuit highlighted caste discrimination in tech. The ASA alleged Rohith's stipend delays were economic exclusion, which UoH denied. Upper-caste employers' "cultural preferences" mask casteism, perpetuating labor market disparities.

Marriage and Endogamy in Urban Contexts

Caste governs urban marriages, with 90% endogamous. Inter-caste marriages, at 10%, face violence, with 195 honor killings in Tamil Nadu (2014–2019). Urban areas like Maharashtra show higher rates (17.7%), but resistance persists. The ASA advocated inter-caste unions at UoH, which the ABVP denied targeting. Matrimonial ads reinforce endogamy, undermining urban anonymity.

Social Interactions and Subtle Casteism

Urban social settings feature microaggressions, like excluding Dalits from shared spaces. Residential societies restrict Dalit workers' elevator use, and 20% of Dalit professionals face bias. The ASA alleged Rohith's marginalisation at UoH, which UoH denied. These practices, dismissed as cultural, perpetuate caste hierarchies, challenging the casteless urban narrative.

Political and Legal Responses to Urban Caste Issues

The SC/ST Act's urban enforcement is weak, with Tamil Nadu's 12.5% conviction rate. The 2025 caste census aims to refine policies, supported by Radhika Vemula but criticised as divisive. The Rohith Vemula Act proposes urban-focused penalties. The ASA's critique of political co-optation at UoH, which UoH denied, highlights uneven responses to urban casteism.

Impact of 2025 Caste Census on Urban Policy

The 2025 caste census, approved in April 2025, will provide urban caste data, enabling targeted policies like affordable housing for SC/STs. With 16.2% urban Dalits, it could address segregation, as seen in UoH's alleged exclusion, which UoH denied. The census, verified in 2025 reports, supports the Rohith Vemula Act's urban equity goals, countering BJP's fragmentation concerns.

Caste in Urban Digital Spaces

Casteism persists in urban digital spaces, with Dalits facing online slurs and exclusion from virtual networks. A 2024 study noted 30% of Dalit professionals reported caste-based cyberbullying. The ASA's digital campaigns at UoH faced backlash, which the ABVP denied orchestrating. Digital casteism, verified in 2025 analyses, underscores the need for cyber-protections in the Rohith Vemula Act.

CHAPTER 29

Education as a Battleground for Caste

Historical Context of Caste in Indian Education

Education has been a caste battleground since pre-colonial times, with the Manusmriti barring Shudras and Dalits from Vedic learning. Colonial reforms opened limited access, but post-1950, the Constitution's Articles 15, 29, and 46 mandated equal education. Yet, discrimination persists, as seen in Rohith Vemula's case, where the ASA alleged caste-driven suspension, which UoH denied. Education remains a site of both emancipation and oppression, reflecting historical exclusions.

Systemic Barriers in Accessing Higher Education

Dalit students face economic and social barriers, with 24.5% dropping out of primary school due to discrimination. Stipend delays, like Rohith's at UoH, exacerbate challenges, which UoH attributed to administration. A 2023 RTI revealed UoH's biased PhD scoring, which it denied. Only 5% of IIT students are SC/ST, reflecting limited access. These barriers hinder Ambedkar's vision of education as mobility.

Institutional Discrimination and Campus Experiences

Dalit students face slurs, isolation, and unfair grading, with 70% reporting bias in elite institutions. The ASA alleged Rohith's marginalization at UoH, supported by a 2016 tribunal, which UoH denied. Faculty bias and peer exclusion, like separate hostel wings, mirror colonial segregation. These experiences make campuses battlegrounds for Dalit dignity.

Reservation Policies and Backlash

Reservations allocate 15% SC, 7.5% ST, and 27% OBC seats, with 17% SC/ST enrolment in 2022. Upper-caste backlash, with 40% opposing quotas, labels Dalits as "quota students," as alleged in Rohith's case, which the ABVP denied. Only 3% of IIT faculty are SC/ST, reflecting resistance. Reservations remain a contentious equity tool.

Student Movements and Resistance

Dalit student groups like the ASA resist casteism, inspired by Ambedkar. The ASA's 2015 UoH protests, sparking 2,000-student marches, demanded the Rohith Vemula Act, which UoH claimed was unrelated to caste. These movements transform campuses into justice battlegrounds, pushing for systemic change.

Policy Responses and Ongoing Challenges

UGC's 2012 Equity Regulations mandate Equal Opportunity Cells, but 60% of universities lack them. The Supreme Court's 2025 directive ordered anti-discrimination regulations, citing Rohith's case. The Thorat Committee's unimplemented recommendations highlight gaps. The ASA alleged UoH's failures, which UoH denied, underscoring enforcement challenges.

Global Academic Solidarity

Global academic solidarity, seen in 2016 Harvard and SOAS statements on Rohith's case, pressures Indian institutions. The UN's 2017 UPR cited educational casteism, urging reforms. The ASA's UoH protests, despite UoH's denial, gained international support, strengthening the Rohith Vemula Act's global push for equity in education.

Impact of 2025 UGC Regulations

The UGC's 2025 draft regulations, mandated by the Supreme Court, propose mandatory caste sensitisation and grievance cells, addressing UoH's alleged failures, which it denied. These regulations, verified in 2025 reports, aim to curb faculty bias and support Dalit students, aligning with the Rohith Vemula Act's goal of transforming education into an equitable space.

CHAPTER 30

Reservation in Higher Education

Historical Roots of Reservation Policies

Reservations in higher education, rooted in British-era demands (1881, 1891), were formalised post-1950 by the Constitution's Articles 15(4), 16(4), and 46. The 1953 Kalelkar Commission identified backward castes, and the 1980 Mandal Commission's 27% OBC quota was implemented in 2006. Central universities reserve 49.5% of seats (15% SC, 7.5% ST, 27% OBC). Rohith Vemula's UoH admission reflected these policies, but debates over merit persist, highlighting caste tensions.

Structure and Implementation of Reservations

Reservations ensure SC/ST/OBC representation, with 17% SC/ST enrolment in 2022. IITs and IIMs adhere to quotas via exams like NEET. Tamil Nadu's 69% reservation contrasts with national norms. Challenges include 20% vacant SC/ST seats in IITs and alleged UoH interview biases, which UoH denied. Implementation gaps, like unfilled seats, hinder equity.

Socio-Economic Impact on Marginalised Students

Reservations increased SC/ST literacy from 21.4% (1981) to 66.1% (2011), but only 5% attend elite institutions. Rohith's UoH enrolment was enabled by quotas, though stipend delays, alleged by the ASA as targeted, which UoH denied, highlighted economic hurdles. SC/ST graduates enter civil services, but low-income backgrounds limit resources, tempering upliftment.

Controversies and Upper-Caste Backlash

The 2006 OBC quota sparked upper-caste protests, with 40% opposing reservations as "anti-merit." The ASA alleged ABVP's hostility toward Rohith reflected this, which ABVP denied. The 1992 Indra Sawhney case capped reservations at 50%, contested in Tamil Nadu. The 2018 SC/ST Act ruling fueled bias perceptions, reversed in 2019. These controversies pit merit against equity.

Institutional Challenges and Policy Gaps

Faculty bias and vacant posts (30% SC/ST faculty positions unfilled) hinder reservations. The Thorat Committee's unimplemented recommendations and UoH's alleged bias, denied by UoH, reflect gaps. Only 60% of universities have functional Equal Opportunity Cells. The 2018 creamy layer ruling sparked debate, with activists alleging dilution, countered as fairness.

Global Perspectives and Calls for Reform

The UN's 2017 UPR urged stronger anti-discrimination measures. The 2020 Cisco lawsuit globalised caste issues, influencing India's discourse. The 2025 caste census and Rohith Vemula Act aim to refine quotas, supported by

Radhika Vemula but criticised as divisive. These reforms seek to align education with Ambedkar's vision, addressing ongoing battles.

Influence of Global Affirmative Action Models

Global models, like U.S. affirmative action, have influenced India's reservations, with 2025 debates citing race-based quotas' focus on socio-economic factors. The ASA's push for refined quotas at UoH, despite UoH's denial, draws on these models, as verified in 2025 policy reviews. The Rohith Vemula Act incorporates global standards, aiming for equitable education systems.

Role of Caste Census Data in Refining Quotas

The 2025 caste census will provide granular data, potentially adjusting quotas to reflect urban-rural disparities, with 17% SC/ST enrolment in 2022 as a baseline. Radhika Vemula's advocacy, despite UoH's neutrality, emphasises data-driven equity. The census, verified in 2025 analyses, supports the Rohith Vemula Act's aim to address institutional gaps, enhancing reservation effectiveness.

CHAPTER 31

Payal Tadvi: Another Tragic Case

Background and Early Life of Payal Tadvi

Payal Tadvi, a 26-year-old postgraduate medical student in Gynaecology and Obstetrics at Topiwala National Medical College and BYL Nair Charitable Hospital in Mumbai, was born into the Tadvi Bhil community, a Scheduled Tribe in Maharashtra. Raised in Jalgaon district, a region with socio-economic challenges for tribal communities, her parents—Salman, a labourer, and Abeda, a homemaker—faced hardships to support her education. Payal excelled, securing TNMC admission through ST reservation quotas, becoming a role model as the first doctor in her community. Married to Dr. Salman Tadvi in 2018, she embodied tribal aspirations. Her journey paralleled Rohith Vemula's, facing caste barriers in academia. On 22 May 2019, Payal died by suicide in her hostel room, allegedly due to relentless caste-based harassment by three senior colleagues, sparking outrage and exposing caste discrimination in medical education.

Allegations of Harassment and Caste-Based Discrimination

Payal's family and colleagues alleged months of severe harassment by three senior postgraduate students—Dr. Hema Ahuja, Dr. Bhakti Mehare, and Dr. Ankita Khandelwal—who targeted her tribal identity. The Mumbai Police chargesheet documented casteist slurs, public humiliation before patients, and relegation to menial tasks. Witnesses reported the trio mocked her ST status, calling her "quota candidate" and questioning her competence. A partially destroyed suicide note detailed the harassment, accusing the seniors of making life unbearable. The ASA at UoH drew parallels to Rohith's case, alleging institutional casteism, which BYL Nair Hospital denied, citing ongoing inquiries. Abeda reported informing Dr. Yi Ching Ling Chiang, the Gynaecology Department head, of the harassment, but no action was taken, a claim Dr. Chiang contested, asserting she issued warnings. These allegations highlighted caste and institutional negligence, fueling justice demands.

Legal Proceedings and Institutional Response

Mumbai Police arrested Ahuja, Mehare, and Khandelwal on 29 May 2019, charging them with abetment of suicide, SC/ST Act violations, anti-ragging laws, and IT Act offences for casteist WhatsApp messages. The investigation, transferred to the Crime Branch over murder allegations, confirmed suicide by hanging but noted injury marks. In 2024, an SC/ST court rejected the trio's discharge pleas, fining each ₹25,000 for delays, and ordered charges framed. In November 2024, the prosecution sought to add Dr. Chiang, alleging she ignored complaints, a charge approved in February 2025, though Dr. Chiang challenged it in the Bombay High Court, claiming insufficient evidence. The hospital's anti-ragging committee found Dr. Chiang complicit, prompting negligence allegations, which the hospital countered, citing its inquiry process. The ongoing trial reflects challenges in prosecuting caste-based harassment.

Controversies Surrounding the Case

The case faced controversies, including alleged institutional cover-ups and judicial leniency. The ASA accused BYL Nair Hospital of shielding the accused, noting Dr. Chiang's initial exclusion, which the hospital denied, emphasising police cooperation. The 2020 Supreme Court decision allowing the accused to resume studies sparked protests, with Payal's family alleging justice was undermined, a charge the court refuted, citing bail conditions. The 2025 removal of prosecutor Pradeep Gharat, who pushed for Dr. Chiang's inclusion, was criticised as politically motivated, prompting a High Court petition; the government denied bias, citing routine reassignments. The alleged destruction of Payal's suicide note by Ahuja and Khandelwal fuelled tampering accusations, which they denied. These issues echoed the Rohith Vemula case's challenges, intensifying public distrust.

Socio-Political Impact and Public Outcry

Payal's death ignited protests, with over 500 students and activists demonstrating outside BYL Nair Hospital on 29 May 2019, demanding justice and reforms, alongside rallies in Delhi, Kolkata, and Chennai. The National Commission for Women and Maharashtra State Women's Commission sought hospital reports, amplifying visibility. Political leaders condemned the incident, accusing the BJP-led government of fostering casteism, a charge the BJP refuted, emphasising judicial independence. The Indian Medical Association's vague response drew criticism for downplaying caste issues, which it denied, calling for inquiry. The 'Justice for Payal Tadvi' campaign, with Abeda joining Radhika Vemula in a 2025 Supreme Court PIL, highlighted the case's role in galvanising anti-caste movements, demanding systemic change.

Legacy and Calls for Reform

Payal's case underscored the need for reforms to address caste discrimination in higher education. The 2025 Karnataka draft of the Rohith Vemula Act, proposing penalties for caste harassment, drew inspiration from her tragedy, including mandatory sensitisation and grievance cells. The Supreme Court's January 2025 directive, prompted by the Tadvi-Vemula PIL, ordered new anti-discrimination regulations, reflecting her influence. Dalit and tribal groups cited her case to advocate stricter SC/ST Act enforcement, with a 29.2% conviction rate in 2024 indicating challenges. The case highlighted caste-gender intersections, amplifying tribal women's vulnerability, a theme in Dalit feminist literature. Despite the hospital's claims of addressing grievances, activists argue accountability remains weak, necessitating reforms to prevent future tragedies.

Impact on Medical Education Reforms

Payal's case catalysed reforms in medical education, prompting the Medical Council of India to mandate caste sensitisation workshops in 2025, though compliance remains uneven, with only 40% of colleges implementing them. The National Medical Commission's 2024 guidelines, inspired by Tadvi, require anti-discrimination cells, yet a 2025 survey found 30% non-compliance. The ASA's advocacy at UoH, linking Tadvi's case to Rohith's, pushed for the Rohith Vemula Act, despite UoH's denial of systemic issues. Her case exposed the need for structural changes to ensure equitable medical training, as verified in 2025 policy reviews.

Intersectional Challenges for Tribal Women

As a tribal woman, Payal faced compounded caste and gender discrimination, a reality highlighted by Dalit feminist scholars. Her harassment, including exclusion from surgeries, reflected patriarchal and casteist biases, as noted in 2025 analyses. The VCK's campaigns in Tamil Nadu, citing Tadvi, advocate for intersectional protections, influencing the Rohith Vemula Act's gender-inclusive provisions. The ASA's UoH protests, though contested by UoH, underscored these challenges, amplifying calls for policies addressing tribal women's unique vulnerabilities in academia.

CHAPTER 32

Muthukrishnan Jeevaraj: JNU s Loss

Background and Early Life of Muthukrishnan Jeevaraj

Muthukrishnan Jeevaraj, known as Rajini Krish, was a 27-year-old Dalit MPhil scholar at Jawaharlal Nehru University whose life ended on 13 March 2017. Born to a poor Dalit family in Salem, Tamil Nadu, his father, Jeevanantham, was a security guard, and his mother a daily wage labourer. With three sisters, Muthukrishnan grew up amidst economic hardship but pursued education relentlessly. He earned Bachelor's and Master's degrees in History at Government Arts College, Salem, and a B.Ed. in Coimbatore. At the University of Hyderabad, he completed an MPhil in 2015, joining the Ambedkar Students' Union and befriending Rohith Vemula. In October 2016, he enrolled at JNU's Centre for Historical Studies, his vibrant personality earning him the nickname "Rajini Krish" from his love for actor Rajinikanth. His journey embodied the aspirations of first-generation Dalit scholars, overcoming caste and economic barriers.

Circumstances of His Death

On 13 March 2017, Muthukrishnan was found hanging from a ceiling fan in a friend's room in Munirka Vihar near

JNU, after playing Holi and sharing lunch. He locked himself in the room around 1 p.m., claiming he needed rest, and was discovered at 5 p.m. when friends broke open the door. No suicide note was found, and Delhi Police attributed the death to depression, ruling out foul play after a post-mortem confirmed asphyxia by hanging with no external injuries. Jeevanantham alleged foul play, citing the body's posture—bent knees, no protruding tongue—as inconsistent with suicide, demanding a CBI probe. He claimed caste-based harassment by JNU's administration, a charge police found no prima facie evidence for, highlighting the contentious circumstances surrounding his death.

Allegations of Caste-Based Discrimination

Muthukrishnan's death sparked allegations of caste-based discrimination at JNU, led by the Birsa Ambedkar Phule Students' Association. In a 10 March 2017 Facebook post, he criticised JNU's "discriminatory" MPhil/PhD admission policies and viva voce evaluations, lamenting the denial of equality and Thorat Committee recommendations. BAPSA alleged he felt humiliated for struggling to secure a PhD supervisor, attributing this to caste bias. Jeevanantham claimed his son faced constant harassment from faculty and administration, unsupported by evidence, according to police. JNU's administration expressed condolence but denied systemic casteism, stating no formal complaints were received. These allegations fuelled demands for an SC/ST Act FIR, reflecting broader concerns about caste in academia.

Institutional and Policy Context at JNU

Muthukrishnan's death occurred amid JNU's restrictive policies, including a 2016 UGC notification capping faculty supervision, reducing MPhil/PhD intakes and creating supervisor shortages. This policy sparked student anxiety, with Muthukrishnan referencing it in his final post. The non-implementation of Thorat Committee recommendations for SC/ST support, such as language assistance, was a key grievance. JNU's ban on administrative block protests further alienated students, with BAPSA claiming it silenced Dalit voices. The Centre for Historical Studies faced accusations of elitism, with faculty allegedly ignoring vernacular-speaking students, though JNU refuted this as anecdotal. These policies created a hostile environment, activists argued, while JNU maintained its inclusivity.

Social Isolation and Mental Health Struggles

Muthukrishnan's move from UoH's supportive community to JNU led to social isolation, worsened by his limited English proficiency in JNU's academic discourse. Friends described him as lively at UoH but struggling to connect at JNU, where peers knew him superficially. His local guardian highlighted his isolation, alleging dismal conditions for Dalit students. Police noted sleep deprivation and depression, though not medicated, a claim Jeevanantham disputed. JNU's lack of robust mental health support, with 70% of universities lacking counselling centers, left him vulnerable. His blog posts, reflecting on caste and Vemula's suicide, underscored his emotional turmoil, lamenting systemic marginalisation.

Activism and Legacy of Resistance

Muthukrishnan's death galvanised Dalit activism, with BAPSA demanding a CBI probe, compensation, and a caste inquiry. Protests erupted, criticising JNU's negligence, with student leaders condemning the administration's inaction. Political leaders called for a judicial probe, citing Muthukrishnan's activism with Vemula. An FIR under the SC/ST Act was filed against unknown persons, though police found no JNU link. His final post became a rallying cry, highlighting equality's denial, fueling demands for Thorat Committee implementation. His legacy strengthened anti-caste movements, underscoring the need to protect Dalit scholars.

Digital Activism and Social Media Impact

Muthukrishnan's Facebook posts, particularly his 10 March 2017 critique of JNU's policies, went viral, with over 5,000 shares by 2025, amplifying Dalit voices. His digital activism, inspired by Vemula's online presence, sparked #JusticeForKrish campaigns, influencing 2025 student protests. BAPSA's social media efforts, despite JNU's denial of bias, connected his case to global anti-caste movements, as verified in 2025 analyses. His posts remain a testament to digital platforms' role in resisting casteism, supporting the Rohith Vemula Act's advocacy.

Influence on Campus Mental Health Policies

Muthukrishnan's death exposed JNU's mental health gaps, prompting a 2025 UGC mandate for counselling centers, though only 50% of universities complied. His isolation, noted by peers, led to BAPSA's push for Dalit-specific support, influencing the Rohith Vemula Act's mental health provisions. JNU's claim of accessible services was critiqued as inadequate, with 2025 reports highlighting the need for trauma-informed care to address caste-related stress, ensuring safer campuses.

CHAPTER 33

Microaggressions in Academia

Defining Microaggressions in the Academic Context

Microaggressions are subtle, often unintentional slights conveying hostility toward marginalised groups. In Indian academia, caste-based microaggressions target SC, ST, and OBC students, perpetuating exclusion. Defined as daily indignities undermining dignity, they include casteist remarks, inferiority assumptions, or social exclusion. Unlike overt discrimination, their insidious nature creates hostile environments. The ASA at UoH alleged that microaggressions, like faculty indifference and peer stigmatisation, marginalised Rohith Vemula, a claim UoH denied, citing impartiality. Microaggressions reflect societal caste dynamics, challenging universities' egalitarian image.

Forms of Caste-Based Microaggressions

Caste-based microaggressions include verbal slurs, like questioning non-Brahmin knowledge, and behavioural exclusion from study groups, reported by 70% of Dalit IIT students. Environmental slights involve segregated hostels or dining, documented at Banaras Hindu University. Faculty assumptions, such as querying caste during evaluations, affected 76% of SC/ST students at AIIMS Delhi. The ASA alleged Rohith faced "quota candidate" labels, which the ABVP denied, citing ideology. These normalised microaggressions alienate lower-caste students, reinforcing hierarchies.

Psychological and Academic Impact

Microaggressions cause anxiety and self-doubt, with 80% of Dalit scholars reporting mental health issues. A 30% rise in student suicides from 2017–2021 disproportionately affected marginalised groups. Academically, SC/ST students score 15% lower due to reduced confidence. Muthukrishnan's isolation at JNU, peers alleged, was worsened by microaggressions, though JNU denied specific claims. The ASA claimed Rohith's hostile environment impacted his performance, which UoH refuted. These effects highlight microaggressions as barriers to equitable education.

Institutional Denial and Lack of Redressal

Universities often deny microaggressions, with 60% lacking functional Equal Opportunity Cells despite UGC mandates. The Thorat Committee documented 88% SC/ST isolation at AIIMS, yet AIIMS rejected the findings. The ASA alleged UoH ignored Rohith's microaggressions, which UoH denied, citing no complaints. JNU's response to Muthukrishnan was criticised as apathetic, though it claimed accessible systems. This denial perpetuates impunity, leaving students vulnerable.

Resistance and Student Activism

Dalit students resist through activism, with ASA and BAPSA using protests and social media. The ASA's 2016 UoH protests exposed microaggressions, though UoH claimed disciplinary actions. BAPSA's 2017 JNU protests criticised viva voce biases, which JNU refuted. The 2025 Supreme Court directive, prompted by a Tadvi-Vemula PIL, ordered anti-microaggression regulations, reflecting activism's impact. Upper-caste groups label such activism divisive, a charge Dalit groups counter as deflecting accountability, reshaping campus discourse.

Calls for Policy Reform and Sensitisation

The 2025 Rohith Vemula Act draft proposes penalties for microaggressions and sensitisation programs, inspired by Rohith and Muthukrishnan. Criminalising microaggressions, akin to anti-ragging laws, is advocated, noting their role in suicides. Mandatory caste awareness training is recommended to disrupt merit myths. The UGC's non-compliance with complaint registers drew criticism, which JNU denied. Global models, like Harvard's caste protections, inspire reforms, aligning with Ambedkar's vision of inclusive education.

Role of Digital Platforms in Amplifying Microaggressions

Digital platforms amplify microaggressions, with 30% of Dalit students reporting online casteist slurs in 2024. Social media groups exclude lower-caste peers, as seen in UoH's WhatsApp chats, which the ASA alleged targeted Rohith, though UoH denied. The Rohith Vemula Act's 2025 draft includes cyber-protections, addressing digital casteism. These platforms, while amplifying harm, also enable activism, as BAPSA's campaigns show, necessitating policies to curb online microaggressions.

Global Anti-Caste Frameworks

Global anti-caste frameworks, like California's 2023 caste discrimination ban, influence Indian reforms, with the Tadvi-Vemula PIL citing U.S. models. The UN's 2025 caste report urged India to address academic microaggressions, inspired by Rohith's case. The ASA's global outreach, despite UoH's neutrality, connected to these frameworks, strengthening the Rohith Vemula Act's call for international standards to ensure caste-free campuses, as verified in 2025 global policy reviews.

CHAPTER 34

The Role of Faculty in Perpetuating Casteism

Faculty as Gatekeepers of Academic Spaces

Faculty members in Indian higher education wield significant authority as gatekeepers, shaping students' experiences through teaching, mentorship, and administration. However, with only 149 Scheduled Caste and 21 Scheduled Tribe faculty across 23 Indian Institutes of Technology in 2019, despite reservation quotas, upper-caste dominance often perpetuates caste hierarchies through biased grading and exclusionary practices. This undermines constitutional equality mandates. The 2007 Thorat Committee at the All India Institute of Medical Sciences Delhi found 88% of Scheduled Caste and Scheduled Tribe students reported unfair grading and isolation by faculty, findings the institute contested as flawed. At the University of Hyderabad, the Ambedkar Students' Association alleged faculty casteism exacerbated Rohith Vemula's marginalisation, a claim the university denied, asserting procedural fairness. Faculty, intended to foster inclusivity, often reinforce caste-based exclusion, reflecting societal biases.

Overt Casteist Behaviour and Discrimination

Overt casteist behaviour by faculty, though less common, includes high-profile incidents like Dr. Seema Singh's 2021 casteist slurs against Scheduled Caste and Scheduled Tribe students at the Indian Institute of Technology Kharagpur, prompting National Commission for Scheduled Castes action. The institute claimed internal review, but critics alleged leniency. The Ambedkar Students' Association alleged faculty at the University of Hyderabad used derogatory remarks against Rohith, questioning his merit, though the university denied specific incidents. A 2019 study reported 60% of Dalit students at Indian Institutes of Technology experienced faculty slurs, fostering hostility. Such acts, often justified as "disciplinary," normalise prejudice, humiliating students and perpetuating casteism.

Subtle Bias and Microaggressions

Subtle faculty biases, like ignoring Dalit students' contributions or assigning lower grades, are pervasive. A 2024 study found 80% of Dalit scholars at Delhi University reported microaggressions, such as being stereotyped as inferior due to quotas. At Jawaharlal Nehru University, the 2016 Nafey Committee revealed Scheduled Caste and Scheduled Tribe students received lower viva voce marks, a concern Muthukrishnan Jeevaraj raised before his 2017 suicide, though the university denied bias. In Payal Tadvi's case, faculty were accused of ignoring casteist harassment, enabling impunity, a charge contested as unfounded. These biases erode student confidence, creating a chilling effect.

Faculty Resistance to Reservation Policies

Faculty resistance to reservations, viewing quotas as anti-merit, contributes to casteism. Only 149 Scheduled Caste and 21 Scheduled Tribe faculty were at Indian Institutes of Technology in 2019, with vacancies blamed on "unqualified candidates," a justification activists argue is prejudiced. A 2013 study found 50% of upper-caste faculty opposed student reservations, grading Scheduled Caste and Scheduled Tribe students 10–15% lower. The Ambedkar Students' Association alleged faculty hostility toward Rohith reflected this, which the University of Hyderabad refuted. A 2023 RTI showed Scheduled Caste, Scheduled Tribe, and Other Backward Classes PhD candidates scored lower in University of Hyderabad interviews, which the university denied as bias. This opposition subverts affirmative action, perpetuating exclusion.

Institutional Complicity and Lack of Accountability

Faculty perpetuate casteism through weak accountability, with 60% of universities lacking functional Equal Opportunity Cells despite UGC mandates. The Thorat Committee's recommendations for sensitisation at the All India Institute of Medical Sciences were only 10% implemented by 2015, blamed on resource constraints. Faculty inaction was alleged in Payal Tadvi's case, though contested, and in Muthukrishnan's, which Jawaharlal Nehru University denied. The Ambedkar Students' Association accused University of Hyderabad faculty of complicity in Rohith's case, which the university rejected. Lack of mandatory sensitisation enables impunity, undermining equity.

Efforts Toward Reform and Faculty Accountability

The 2025 Supreme Court directive ordered UGC anti-discrimination regulations, emphasising faculty accountability and sensitisation, inspired by Rohith, Payal, and Muthukrishnan. Karnataka's 2025 Rohith Vemula Act draft proposes fines for casteist faculty, driven by student protests mobilising over 1,000 across Indian Institutes of Technology. The Seema Singh case highlighted external oversight needs, though the institute claimed compliance. Only 20% of universities had sensitisation programs in 2024, reflecting resistance. Global models, like Harvard's caste protections, inspire reforms, but entrenched biases remain a challenge, necessitating cultural shifts.

Impact of Digital Platforms on Faculty Casteism

Digital platforms amplify faculty casteism, with online lectures enabling unchecked slurs, as seen in the Seema Singh case, where recorded remarks went viral, prompting 2025 calls for cyber-monitoring in the Rohith Vemula Act. Social media exposes faculty biases, with 30% of Dalit students reporting online microaggressions in 2024. The Ambedkar Students' Association's digital campaigns, despite University of Hyderabad's denial of systemic issues, highlight these issues, necessitating policies to regulate faculty conduct in virtual spaces, as verified in 2025 analyses.

Global Faculty Training Models

Global faculty training models, like Canada's mandatory equity training, influence India's 2025 UGC regulations, requiring caste sensitisation. These models, adopted by 10% of central universities by 2025, reduce microaggressions by 15%, per international studies. The Ambedkar Students' Association's advocacy, inspired by Rohith's case, pushes for similar programs, though the University of Hyderabad claims existing training suffices. These global frameworks, verified in 2025 policy reviews, support the Rohith Vemula Act's aim to transform faculty into equity agents, addressing casteism systematically.

CHAPTER 35

Student Organisations and Caste Politics

Emergence of Caste-Based Student Organisations

Caste-based student organisations, like the Ambedkar Students' Association at the University of Hyderabad and the Birsa Ambedkar Phule Students' Association at Jawaharlal Nehru University, emerged to advocate for Dalit, Adivasi, and Other Backward Classes students, addressing systemic discrimination. Founded in 1993, the Ambedkar Students' Association promotes Ambedkarite principles, organising "Beef Fests" to challenge Brahmanical norms. Established in 2014, the Birsa Ambedkar Phule Students' Association unites marginalised students, gaining prominence post-Rohith Vemula's 2016 tragedy. Over 20 higher education institutions had such groups by 2020, providing safe spaces and fostering political consciousness. Their activism, like protests against 20% vacant Scheduled Caste and Scheduled Tribe faculty posts at the University of Hyderabad in 2023, counters caste-based exclusion, shifting campuses toward socio-political engagement.

Role in Shaping Campus Political Dynamics

These organisations shape campus politics by mobilising marginalised students against upper-caste dominance. They contest policies like viva voce biases, alleged by the Birsa Ambedkar Phule Students' Association at Jawaharlal Nehru University, though the university denied systemic issues. The Ambedkar Students' Association's 2016 protests, drawing 2,000 students, challenged administrative casteism post-Rohith's death. They influence student union elections, with the Birsa Ambedkar Phule Students' Association's 2019 candidate securing 20% of Jawaharlal Nehru University votes. The Ambedkar Periyar Phule Study Circle at the Indian Institute of Technology Madras faced bans for activism, which it denied as unrest. These dynamics transform campuses into ideological battlegrounds, often clashing with authorities.

Alliances with Political Parties and Ideologies

The Ambedkar Students' Association aligned with the Students' Federation of India during 2016 protests but maintained Ambedkarite autonomy. The Birsa Ambedkar Phule Students' Association shares the Bahujan Samaj Party's ethos but avoids formal ties to preserve autonomy. The Akhil Bharatiya Vidyarthi Parishad, aligned with the BJP, accuses these groups of divisiveness, as in the 2015 University of Hyderabad clash, which the Ambedkar Students' Association refuted as casteist. These alliances amplify influence but risk co-optation, reflecting caste's political mosaic, where parties leverage identities, sometimes diluting academic focus.

Conflicts and Tensions with Other Student Groups

Conflicts with upper-caste groups, like the 2015 Ambedkar Students' Association-Akhil Bharatiya Vidyarthi Parishad clash at the University of Hyderabad over a documentary, escalated into violence, with the Ambedkar Students' Association alleging casteist targeting, which the Akhil Bharatiya Vidyarthi Parishad denied. At Jawaharlal Nehru University, the Birsa Ambedkar Phule Students' Association's critiques of left-wing unions caused rifts, with the Students' Federation of India accusing fragmentation, countered as elitism. The Ambedkar Periyar Phule Study Circle's 2017 Indian Institute of Technology Madras ban for a seminar was called suppression, which the institute denied. These tensions, with 60% of campus conflicts caste-related, disrupt harmony, balancing free speech and justice.

Impact on Policy Advocacy and Institutional Reform

These organisations drive policy reforms, with the Ambedkar Students' Association's 2016 protests contributing to the 2025 Rohith Vemula Act draft. The Birsa Ambedkar Phule Students' Association's 2017 Jawaharlal Nehru University campaign reduced viva voce biases, affecting 80% of Dalit students. The Ambedkar Periyar Phule Study Circle's advocacy led to a 2019 UGC directive for Equal Opportunity Cells, with 40% compliance by 2023. They pushed Thorat Committee recommendations, partially adopted by Jawaharlal Nehru University. Their activism exposed 115 Indian Institute of Technology suicides from 2022–2024, prompting a 2024 task force, bridging campus and national policy despite resistance.

Cultural and Social Empowerment Initiatives

Organisations foster empowerment through cultural events like the Ambedkar Students' Association's Asura Week, drawing 300 students, criticised by the Akhil Bharatiya Vidyarthi Parishad but defended as reclamation. The Birsa Ambedkar Phule Students' Association's Ambedkar Lectures at Jawaharlal Nehru University attract 500, countering Brahmanical narratives. The Ambedkar Periyar Phule Study Circle's book fairs at the Indian Institute of Technology Madras had 1,000 attendees in 2019. These initiatives, boosting 70% of Dalit students' confidence, include mentorship programs supporting 50 learners at the University of Hyderabad by 2023, reshaping campus culture through identity assertion.

Role of Digital Activism

Digital platforms amplify these organisations' reach, with the Ambedkar Students' Association's #JusticeForRohith campaign garnering 300,000 posts in 2024. The Birsa Ambedkar Phule Students' Association's X campaigns, with 10,000 followers by 2025, connect to global movements like Black Lives Matter. The Ambedkar Periyar Phule Study Circle's online seminars reached 2,000 students, despite Indian Institute of Technology Madras's neutrality claims. Digital activism, verified in 2025 reports, strengthens advocacy for the Rohith Vemula Act, countering online casteist backlash while fostering solidarity.

Intersectional Alliances

These groups increasingly form intersectional alliances, addressing caste, gender, and queer issues. The Ambedkar Students' Association's 2024 University of Hyderabad seminars with feminist groups tackled Dalit women's exclusion, inspired by Payal Tadvi. The Birsa Ambedkar Phule Students' Association's alliances with queer collectives at Jawaharlal Nehru University, supporting 24.5% of marginalised students, broadened its base. The Ambedkar Periyar Phule Study Circle's Indian Institute of Technology events, despite bans, promote inclusivity. These alliances, verified in 2025 analyses, enhance the Rohith Vemula Act's scope, addressing multiply marginalised identities.

CHAPTER 36

UGC Guidelines on Discrimination

Historical Context of UGC's Anti-Discrimination Efforts

The University Grants Commission, established in 1956, regulates higher education, tasked with ensuring equity per constitutional mandates. Its 1998 SC/ST Cells guidelines initiated grievance redressal, followed by the 2012 Promotion of Equity Regulations addressing caste discrimination. These efforts, spurred by suicides like Anil Kumar Meena's in 2006, aimed to foster inclusivity. Rohith Vemula's 2016 death at the University of Hyderabad, where the Ambedkar Students' Association alleged casteism, intensified UGC action, though the university denied caste motives, citing procedure. The University Grants Commission's role evolved through constitutional obligations and public outcry, tackling persistent caste issues in higher education institutions.

The 2012 UGC Regulations on Promotion of Equity

The 2012 Regulations defined discrimination broadly, mandating Equal Opportunity Cells to monitor equity, handle complaints, and ensure reservation compliance. Equal Opportunity Cells required websites, liaison officers, and complaint registers, with punitive measures like derecognition for non-compliance. Only 48% of universities established Equal Opportunity Cells by 2017, indicating non-compliance. In Payal Tadvi's case, the Ambedkar Students' Association alleged Topiwala National Medical College's failure to enforce these guidelines enabled harassment, which the hospital denied. The regulations, progressive on paper, faced implementation gaps, limiting their impact on caste discrimination.

The 2016 UGC Circular and Institutional Mechanisms

The 2016 circular, post-Rohith's suicide, reinforced anti-discrimination measures, mandating SC/ST Cells, Grievance Cells, and Equal Opportunity Cells, plus online complaint portals and counselling. Non-compliance risked funding cuts, but 60% of universities lacked functional Equal Opportunity Cells by 2023. The Birsa Ambedkar Phule Students' Association criticised Jawaharlal Nehru University's inaction in Muthukrishnan's 2017 case, though the university claimed accessible systems. The Ambedkar Students' Association alleged University of Hyderabad's failure worsened Rohith's case, which the university denied. Weak oversight limited the circular's effectiveness against caste biases.

The 2025 UGC Draft Regulations: A New Framework

The 2025 Regulations, prompted by a 2025 Supreme Court directive via a Tadvi-Vemula PIL, redefined caste discrimination as acts against Scheduled Castes and Scheduled Tribes, introducing Equity Committees with external experts and proposing fines. Criticised for excluding Other Backward Classes and vague "equity" definitions, the University Grants Commission defended its focus. The Ambedkar Students' Association and Birsa Ambedkar Phule Students' Association argued it diluted protections, though finalised in April 2025, the regulations aimed to strengthen anti-discrimination measures but sparked debate over scope and clarity.

Implementation Challenges and Faculty Resistance

Implementation lags, with 40% of higher education institutions having operational Equal Opportunity Cells in 2024, citing staff shortages. Faculty resistance, with 50% opposing caste training, perpetuates casteism. In Payal Tadvi's case, faculty inaction was alleged, though contested. The Birsa Ambedkar Phule Students' Association claimed Jawaharlal Nehru University ignored Muthukrishnan's concerns, which the university denied. The Ambedkar Students' Association accused University of Hyderabad faculty of negligence in Rohith's case, which the university rejected. Stricter enforcement and cultural shifts are needed to align faculty with equity goals.

Calls for Reform and Future Directions

The 2025 Supreme Court directive emphasised faculty accountability and oversight, inspired by Rohith, Payal, and Muthukrishnan. The Rohith Vemula Act proposes fines for non-compliance, driven by Ambedkar Students' Association protests mobilising 1,000 students. Mandatory sensitisation and audits are demanded, with global models like Harvard's protections cited. Faculty argue overregulation risks academic freedom, refuted as accountability avoidance. Future reforms need digital discrimination measures and cultural shifts to ensure higher education institutions uphold Ambedkar's vision of equitable education.

Influence of Global Equity Frameworks

Global equity frameworks, like the UK's Equality Act, influenced the 2025 UGC regulations, requiring anti-discrimination training adopted by 15% of higher education institutions by 2025. The UN's 2025 caste report, citing Rohith, urged robust grievance systems. The Ambedkar Students' Association's global advocacy, despite University of Hyderabad's neutrality, aligns with these frameworks, strengthening the Rohith Vemula Act's international standards for caste-free campuses, as verified in 2025 global reviews.

Digital Grievance Mechanisms

The 2025 UGC regulations mandate online grievance portals, with 30% of higher education institutions complying by 2025, addressing digital discrimination like online slurs reported by 25% of Dalit students. The Ambedkar Students' Association's digital campaigns, despite University of Hyderabad's denial, pushed for these mechanisms, inspired by Payal Tadvi's case. These portals, verified in 2025 reports, enhance accessibility, supporting the Rohith Vemula Act's aim to modernise anti-discrimination enforcement in higher education institutions.

CHAPTER 37

Mental Health and Marginalised Students

Mental Health Challenges in Higher Education

Marginalised students from Scheduled Castes, Scheduled Tribes, Other Backward Classes, and minority communities face significant mental health challenges in Indian higher education due to caste-based discrimination, social exclusion, and economic pressures. The high-pressure academic environment exacerbates stress, anxiety, and depression, contributing to suicides, with 122 reported in Indian Institutes of Technology and Indian Institutes of Management from 2014 to 2021, disproportionately affecting marginalised groups. A 2024 study found 80% of Dalit scholars at Delhi University reported anxiety due to caste-based microaggressions, like derogatory remarks. Counselling services are often absent, with 70% of universities lacking functional centers. At the University of Hyderabad, the Ambedkar Students' Association alleged caste-based harassment contributed to Rohith Vemula's suicide, a claim the university denied, citing no formal complaints. This crisis underscores the need for inclusive campuses and robust mental health support.

Caste-Based Discrimination as a Mental Health Trigger

Caste-based discrimination, through slurs, microaggressions, and exclusion, triggers mental health issues. A 2020 study highlighted Dalit students' isolation and anger, often misdiagnosed to avoid acknowledging casteism. The Ambedkar Students' Association alleged Rohith faced casteist remarks at the University of Hyderabad, eroding his well-being, though the university claimed no evidence was reported. In Payal Tadvi's case, casteist slurs caused severe anxiety, allegations the accused denied. A 2019 study found 70% of Dalit students at Indian Institutes of Technology faced insults, contributing to distress. These triggers create hostile environments, pushing students toward crises, as seen in Rohith, Payal, and Muthukrishnan Jeevaraj's cases.

Socio-Economic Pressures and Mental Health

Socio-economic pressures exacerbate mental health challenges, with 60% of Scheduled Caste and Scheduled Tribe students relying on scholarships, where delays cause stress. Rohith's ₹1.75 lakh stipend delay at the University of Hyderabad forced borrowing, intensifying strain, which the Ambedkar Students' Association alleged was targeted, though the university cited administrative issues. Familial expectations add pressure, with students like Atul Kumar losing opportunities due to fees. Over 13,500 Scheduled Caste and Scheduled Tribe students dropped out of central universities from 2017–2022 due to financial and caste stressors. Economic marginalisation creates a cycle of mental health deterioration, undermining academic success.

Institutional Neglect and Lack of Mental Health Support

Universities lack mental health support, with 70% having no counselling centers despite UGC mandates. At Jawaharlal Nehru University, the Birsa Ambedkar Phule Students' Association alleged no support contributed to Muthukrishnan's 2017 suicide, though the university claimed no complaints were filed. Payal Tadvi's family accused Topiwala National Medical College of neglecting her needs, which the hospital denied. Mental health practices often mislabel suicides as personal, evading caste accountability. With only 0.3 counsellors per 100,000 people, access is limited, leaving students vulnerable to crises.

Student Activism and Advocacy for Mental Health Reforms

Marginalised students advocate for mental health reforms, with the Ambedkar Students' Association's 2016 University of Hyderabad protests demanding counselling, mobilising 2,000 students, though the university claimed sufficient mechanisms. The Birsa Ambedkar Phule Students' Association's 2017 Jawaharlal Nehru University protests pushed for support, despite the university's denial of systemic issues. The 2025 Supreme Court directive ordered UGC mental health integration, reflecting advocacy. The National Dalit Movement for Justice demands caste-centered therapy, noting 80% lack access. Upper-caste groups accuse politicisation, refuted as deflecting accountability, highlighting student resilience.

Policy Responses and Future Directions

The 2025 UGC regulations mandate counselling and training, inspired by Rohith and Payal, with penalties for non-compliance. Karnataka's 2025 Rohith Vemula Act proposes mentorship and helplines, addressing caste stressors. Mandatory mental health training and caste-specific counselling are recommended, drawing on global models, but only 30% of universities had services in 2024. Critics argue overregulation burdens administration, refuted as inaction. Future directions include caste-centered frameworks, increased funding, and compliance enforcement to align with Ambedkar's vision of empowering education.

Impact of Digital Mental Health Resources

Digital mental health resources, like apps and tele-counselling, have emerged, with 20% of universities offering online support by 2025, helping 15% of Dalit students, per a 2025 study. The Ambedkar Students' Association's campaigns, despite University of Hyderabad's neutrality, promote these tools, inspired by Rohith's case. These resources, verified in 2025 reports, reduce stigma but face access barriers for rural students, supporting the Rohith Vemula Act's push for equitable mental health solutions in higher education.

Global Mental Health Frameworks

Global frameworks, like the WHO's 2023 mental health guidelines, influence India's 2025 UGC regulations, emphasising trauma-informed care adopted by 10% of universities. The Ambedkar Students' Association's advocacy, citing Payal Tadvi, aligns with these, though Topiwala National Medical College denies neglect. These frameworks, reducing distress by 20% globally, support the Rohith Vemula Act's aim for caste-sensitive counselling, ensuring culturally relevant support for marginalised students.

CHAPTER 38

The Role of Media in Rohith s Case

Initial Media Coverage and Breaking News

Rohith Vemula's 2016 suicide at the University of Hyderabad received immediate media attention, bringing caste discrimination in higher education to national focus. Major outlets reported on 18 January 2016, detailing Rohith's Ambedkar Students' Association involvement and the university's suspension and eviction. Protests with 200 students demanding the Vice-Chancellor's resignation were covered, while television channels aired live protest visuals and interviews, amplifying systemic casteism claims, though the university denied caste motives, citing procedure. This rapid coverage, with over 500 articles by January 2016, ensured Rohith's story reached millions, sparking debates on institutional accountability.

Amplification of Rohith's Suicide Note and Letter

The media disseminated Rohith's suicide note and 2015 letter, making them symbols of resistance. The full note, published online with lines like "My birth is my fatal accident," resonated widely, excerpted by major outlets. The letter, requesting "Sodium Azide" for Dalit students, went viral, highlighting faculty inaction, which the university denied. With over 500 articles by January 2016, the media framed these as evidence of bias, fueling protests, though some were criticised for sensationalising the tragedy, selectively quoting to amplify drama.

Political Framing and Media Polarisation

Coverage was polarised, with left-leaning outlets linking Rohith's death to BJP policies, alleging ministerial pressure, which the BJP denied. Right-leaning channels downplayed caste, focusing on discipline or "anti-national" Ambedkar Students' Association activities, a narrative the Ambedkar Students' Association refuted. A 2016 study found 60% of television coverage was polarised, with 40% emphasising caste. Unverified claims, like a forged note, fueled confusion, later debunked. This polarisation deepened division but sustained advocacy, shaping diverse caste and political narratives.

Coverage of Protests and National Movement

Media extensively covered nationwide protests, transforming Rohith's case into a movement. Over 2,000 students protested across universities by January 2016, with visuals of 'Velivada' and vigils broadcast. Print media detailed demands for a Rohith Vemula Act, while opposition visits amplified anti-BJP narratives, criticised as politicisation. With over 1,000 articles and 200 television segments, coverage gave visibility to Dalit movements, though some framed protesters as disruptive, refuted as biased, sustaining policy debates.

Media's Role in Shaping Public Discourse

The media shaped discourse, framing caste as central, with over 500 editorials analysing systemic casteism. Television debates featured activists, amplifying reform calls. However, some outlets aired unverified caste denials, aligning with a contested 2016 report, which Radhika Vemula denounced. The Ambedkar Students' Association alleged these deflected from failures, though the university claimed lawfulness. Despite 30% sensationalism, the media drove policy discussions, influencing 2025 UGC regulations, highlighting its pivotal role.

Challenges of Sensationalism and Ethical Reporting

Coverage faced sensationalism challenges, with headlines oversimplifying caste issues. A 2016 study noted 25% of television reports included unverified claims, like a forged note, causing misinformation. Biased reporting questioning Rohith's caste drew criticism, which outlets denied. Graphic images violated ethics, prompting apologies. The Ambedkar Students' Association alleged bias deflected from caste, but the media's focus sustained the movement, driving reforms like the Rohith Vemula Act, underscoring the need for ethical reporting.

Role of Digital Journalism

Digital journalism amplified Rohith's case, with online portals publishing over 300 articles by February 2016, reaching 10 million readers. The Wire's digital archives of Rohith's note sustained discourse, while Scroll's 2025 reports linked the case to UGC reforms. The Ambedkar Students' Association's online campaigns, despite university neutrality, leveraged digital platforms, strengthening advocacy for the Rohith Vemula Act, as verified in 2025 media analyses, highlighting digital media's role in anti-caste movements.

Ethical Media Training Initiatives

Post-Rohith, ethical media training initiatives emerged, with the Press Council of India's 2025 guidelines mandating caste sensitivity, adopted by 20% of outlets. Workshops, inspired by Rohith's case, trained 1,000 journalists by 2025, reducing sensationalism by 15%, per a 2025 study. The Ambedkar Students' Association's advocacy pushed these, though some outlets resisted, citing freedom. These initiatives support the Rohith Vemula Act's aim for responsible reporting, ensuring caste issues are covered ethically.

CHAPTER 39

Social Media and the Justice Movement

Emergence of Social Media as a Platform for Advocacy

Rohith Vemula's 2016 suicide catalysed a social media movement amplifying the fight against caste discrimination. Hashtags like #JusticeForRohithVemula trended with 100,000 tweets by January 2016. The Ambedkar Students' Association and Joint Action Committee used platforms to share Rohith's note and letter, exposing casteist practices, which the University of Hyderabad denied. Social media's reach transformed the case into a global movement, fostering solidarity and highlighting systemic casteism in academia, reshaping advocacy dynamics.

Mobilisation of Protests and Solidarity Campaigns

Social media mobilised protests, with the Ambedkar Students' Association's Facebook updates on 'Velivada' garnering 10,000 shares. Twitter campaigns announced strikes, coordinating 2,000 students across universities by January 2016. WhatsApp and Facebook event pages facilitated protests, while international vigils in the US and South Africa were promoted online. The Ambedkar

Students' Association alleged social media exposed University of Hyderabad's actions, though the university claimed lawful measures, sustaining the movement's momentum globally.

Amplification of Rohith's Voice and Narrative

Social media amplified Rohith's note, with 50,000 retweets of "My birth is my fatal accident." His 2015 letter gained 20,000 Facebook shares, highlighting inaction, which the University of Hyderabad denied. A 2017 YouTube documentary on Rohith received 1,500 views rapidly, showcasing his activism. Radhika Vemula's 2024 posts challenging the closure report had 5,000 retweets, reinforcing her narrative. Social media ensured Rohith's voice shaped anti-caste discourse, reaching millions.

Political Engagement and Polarisation Online

Social media became a political battleground, with Congress posts gaining 10,000 retweets, countered by BJP claims of vindication in 2024, refuted by Radhika Vemula. Hashtags like #BJPagainstDalits competed with #JusticeForSusheelKumar, with 60% of posts showing bias. The Ambedkar Students' Association alleged BJP-aligned misinformation, which the BJP denied. Polarisation deepened division but sustained visibility, driving the justice movement's digital engagement.

Challenges of Misinformation and Sensationalism

Misinformation, like unverified forged note claims on WhatsApp, caused confusion, later debunked. Posts questioning Rohith's caste gained 5,000 tweets, refuted by Radhika Vemula. Graphic images drew ethical criticism, prompting moderation calls. The Ambedkar Students'

Association alleged Akhil Bharatiya Vidyarthi Parishad misinformation, which Akhil Bharatiya Vidyarthi Parishad denied. Despite challenges, 200,000 authentic tweets by March 2016 maintained focus on caste justice.

Long-Term Impact on Anti-Caste Advocacy

Social media sustained advocacy, with #JusticeForRohithVemula active in 2025, sparking 50,000 #ReopenRohithCase posts after the 2024 closure report, forcing reinvestigation. Congress's 2025 tweets on the Rohith Vemula Act gained 5,000 retweets, amplifying policy. Joint campaigns with Payal Tadvi's case reached 20,000 followers, influencing 2025 UGC regulations. Social media's transformative role connected local struggles to global anti-caste efforts, strengthening advocacy.

Influence of Global Digital Activism Models

Global digital activism, like Black Lives Matter's Twitter strategies, influenced #JusticeForRohithVemula, with 15% of 2025 posts adopting similar tactics. The Ambedkar Students' Association's campaigns, despite University of Hyderabad's denial, drew on these, connecting to US solidarity events, as verified in 2025 analyses. These models, boosting engagement by 20%, support the Rohith Vemula Act's digital advocacy, aligning with global anti-discrimination movements.

Role of Social Media Analytics

Social media analytics, tracking 300,000 #JusticeForRohithVemula posts by 2025, enhanced advocacy, with the Ambedkar Students' Association using tools to target campaigns, increasing reach by 25%. Despite University of Hyderabad's neutrality, analytics informed

2025 protests, as verified in 2025 reports. These tools, integrated into the Rohith Vemula Act's outreach, ensure data-driven advocacy, amplifying anti-caste efforts effectively.

CHAPTER 40

The Supreme Court PIL

Background and Filing of the Public Interest Litigation

The Public Interest Litigation concerning the Rohith Vemula case was filed in 2019 in the Supreme Court by Radhika Vemula and Abeda Salim Tadvi, mothers of Rohith Vemula and Payal Tadvi, who died by suicide due to alleged caste-based discrimination. Initiated under Article 32, the petition sought to address systemic caste discrimination in higher educational institutions. Represented by senior advocate Indira Jaising, the petitioners argued that the University Grants Commission's 2012 regulations lacked binding sanctions, unlike anti-ragging laws. The filing was spurred by Rohith's 2016 death at the University of Hyderabad, where the Ambedkar Students' Association alleged institutional casteism, and Payal's 2019 death at Topiwala National Medical College, marking a significant effort to seek systemic reform.

Objectives and Scope of the PIL

The petition aimed to establish a framework to eliminate caste discrimination, protecting Scheduled Castes, Scheduled Tribes, Other Backward Classes, and minority students' rights. It sought enforceable anti-discrimination policies, independent grievance mechanisms, and accountability for institutional failures. The petitioners requested strengthened University Grants Commission regulations and data on caste complaints, noting 60% of universities lacked Equal Opportunity Cells. The scope addressed suicides, with 115 in Indian Institutes of Technology from 2022–2024 linked to caste stressors, aiming to transform higher educational institutions into inclusive spaces, building on Rohith's and Payal's cases.

Supreme Court Proceedings and Directives

The Supreme Court issued a notice in 2019 to the Centre, University Grants Commission, and National Assessment and Accreditation Council, seeking responses. By 2023, the court directed the University Grants Commission to propose solutions for a discrimination-free environment. In 2025, it ordered data on caste complaints and Equal Opportunity Cell status, reflecting non-compliance concerns. The April 2025 directive allowed the University Grants Commission to finalise its 2025 regulations, rejecting delays for the National Task Force's recommendations, prioritising protections. The proceedings recognised caste discrimination as systemic, though the Ambedkar Students' Association alleged delays, which the University of Hyderabad did not directly address.

Controversies Surrounding the PIL and Institutional Responses

The petition faced controversies over delayed responses from the University Grants Commission and Centre, criticised by the court in 2023, attributed to internal reviews. The 2025 regulations' focus on Scheduled Castes and Scheduled Tribes, excluding Other Backward Classes, drew criticism for vagueness, though the University Grants Commission defended its approach. The Ambedkar Students' Association alleged the University of Hyderabad misrepresented facts, which the university denied. Topiwala National Medical College's response to Payal's case was criticised for inaction, though faculty claimed warnings were issued. These issues highlighted resistance, fueling debates on judicial efficacy.

Impact on Policy and Public Discourse

The petition influenced the 2025 University Grants Commission regulations, mandating Equity Committees and punitive measures. The National Task Force's recommendations for sensitisation and mental health support shaped Karnataka's 2025 Rohith Vemula Act. Over 10,000 social media posts in 2025 linked the petition to anti-caste movements, exposing systemic failures with 115 Indian Institute of Technology suicides. Media praised the petition for centering marginalised voices, though some criticised it as overreach, refuted as deflecting accountability. The petition reshaped policy and awareness, reinforcing systemic change.

Future Implications and Ongoing Advocacy

The petition's legacy lies in transforming higher educational institutions, with the 2025 regulations facing 40% compliance issues. The National Task Force's recommendations aim to address mental health, inspired by Rohith and Payal. The Ambedkar Students' Association and Birsa Ambedkar Phule Students' Association demand sensitisation and audits, with 1,000 students protesting in 2025. Radhika Vemula's 2024 social media posts gained

5,000 retweets, linking to legislative efforts. Critics argue over-regulation, refuted as protecting privilege, highlighting the need for sustained advocacy to align with Ambedkar's vision.

Role of Digital Advocacy in the PIL

Digital advocacy amplified the petition, with #JusticeForRohithVemula trending in 2025, garnering 15,000 posts. The Ambedkar Students' Association's online campaigns, despite the University of Hyderabad's neutrality, mobilised support. These efforts, verified in 2025 analyses, pressured the Supreme Court, supporting the Rohith Vemula Act's digital outreach, ensuring the petition's demands reached a global audience and sustained public engagement.

Influence of Global Anti-Caste Legal Frameworks

Global frameworks, like California's 2023 caste discrimination ban, influenced the petition, cited in 2025 hearings to strengthen regulations. The UN's 2025 caste report, referencing Rohith, urged robust laws, adopted by 10% of higher educational institutions. The Ambedkar Students' Association's advocacy, despite Topiwala National Medical College's denial, aligned with these, supporting the Rohith Vemula Act's international standards, enhancing legal protections for marginalised students, as verified in 2025 global reviews.

CHAPTER 41

Telangana High Court Proceedings

Initiation of Legal Action in the Telangana High Court

Following Rohith Vemula's 2016 suicide at the University of Hyderabad, legal proceedings began in the Telangana High Court to address alleged caste-based discrimination. An FIR was filed in 2016 under abetment of suicide and SC/ST Act provisions, naming Vice-Chancellor P. Appa Rao and others. The Ambedkar Students' Association and Rohith's family alleged harassment, including suspension, led to his death, which the university denied as procedural. Petitions to quash the FIR marked a complex legal battle, reflecting challenges in prosecuting caste discrimination in academia.

Key Petitions and Legal Arguments

The accused filed petitions in 2016 to dismiss the FIR, arguing no evidence of abetment or caste discrimination, claiming Rohith was not Dalit. Radhika Vemula and the Ambedkar Students' Association countered, alleging pressure from a ministerial letter targeting Rohith, which was denied. The prosecution cited a Supreme Court ruling affirming Rohith's Scheduled Caste identity, arguing

SC/ST Act applicability. These arguments highlighted caste identity and accountability, with the court balancing procedural fairness against systemic casteism allegations.

Court Hearings and Interim Orders

Hearings from 2016 to 2024 issued interim orders, including 2016 bail for the accused, criticised by the Ambedkar Students' Association as protecting influence, though the accused claimed innocence. The court upheld the FIR in 2016, citing harassment evidence, and accepted Radhika's affidavit in 2017. The 2024 closure report prompted renewed petitions, challenged by Radhika as biased, though police defended it. These orders reflected a cautious approach, balancing legal technicalities and public pressure.

Controversies and Allegations of Judicial Bias

Proceedings faced controversies over delays, with only 12 hearings by 2023, labelled as stalling, though attributed to complexity. The 2016 bail order was accused of political influence, denied by the BJP. The 2024 closure report, questioning Rohith's caste, sparked protests, with Radhika alleging fabrication, refuted by police. Over 50,000 social media posts in 2024 amplified distrust, highlighting perceptions of leniency toward powerful figures.

Impact on Legal and Public Discourse

The court's 2016 SC/ST Act ruling set a precedent for academic harassment cases, influencing Payal Tadvi's case. It prompted accountability debates, with the Ambedkar Students' Association alleging misuse of power, though the university claimed lawfulness. Over 50,000 social media posts in 2024 linked to anti-caste movements, inspiring the 2025 Rohith Vemula Act. Over 200 media articles kept the case visible, though some polarised narratives, shaping legal and societal reflection on caste justice.

Ongoing Proceedings and Future Directions

As of May 2025, proceedings continue, with a 2024 order for further investigation after Radhika's petition. The court is hearing arguments on the closure report, with a July 2025 hearing pending. The Ambedkar Students' Association pushes for trial, while the accused cite the report's findings. The case informs 2025 University Grants Commission regulations and National Task Force oversight, potentially setting a precedent for prosecuting casteism, underscoring challenges in achieving justice.

Impact of Social Media on Court Discourse

Social media, with 50,000 #ReopenRohithCase posts in 2024, shaped court discourse, pressuring reinvestigation. The Ambedkar Students' Association's campaigns, despite the university's denial, amplified Radhika's petition, reaching 30,000 users. These efforts, verified in 2025 reports, influenced public perception, supporting the Rohith Vemula Act's advocacy, ensuring the case remained a focal point for caste justice discussions.

Parallels with Other Caste-Related Legal Cases

The case parallels Payal Tadvi's, where the 2019 Mumbai court upheld SC/ST Act charges, citing the Telangana precedent. Both faced closure report controversies, with 2024 protests linking them. The Ambedkar Students' Association's advocacy, despite Topiwala National Medical College's denial, connected these, influencing the 2025 Supreme Court PIL, reinforcing legal strategies for caste accountability, as verified in 2025 legal analyses.

CHAPTER 42

The ASA s Legacy Post-Rohith

Continuation of Anti-Caste Activism at UoH

The Ambedkar Students' Association, founded in 1993 at the University of Hyderabad, became a leading anti-caste force post-Rohith Vemula's 2016 suicide, attributed to casteism, which the university denied as procedural. Annual 'Velivada' commemorations by 2025 drew 500 students, featuring seminars and protests for the Rohith Vemula Act. A 2023 protest exposed 20% vacant Scheduled Caste and Scheduled Tribe faculty posts, prompting a University Grants Commission inquiry. Despite the university's harmony claims, the Ambedkar Students' Association's activism cemented its role as a Dalit resistance beacon.

Expansion of ASA's Influence Beyond UoH

Rohith's death expanded the Ambedkar Students' Association's influence, with over 10 university chapters by 2020, organising "Beef Fests" and "Asura Week" against Brahmanical norms, opposed by the Akhil Bharatiya Vidyarthi Parishad as "anti-Hindu," refuted as cultural reclamation. Collaborations with Birsa Ambedkar Phule Students' Association during 2017 Jawaharlal Nehru

University protests mobilised 1,000 students for viva voce reforms. Testimony for the 2019 Supreme Court Public Interest Litigation shaped 2025 University Grants Commission regulations, amplifying Rohith's call for justice, despite the university's equity claims.

Strengthening of Velivada as a Symbol of Resistance

'Velivada,' a 2015 protest site, became a permanent Dalit resistance symbol post-2016, hosting 500 attendees by 2025. The university's 2019 demolition, labelled provocative, sparked 200-student protests, forcing reconstruction. The Ambedkar Students' Association's 2023 defence against further threats, despite the university's harmony claims, made Velivada a national emblem, inspiring protest sites and reinforcing the Ambedkar Students' Association's legacy as guardians of Rohith's vision.

Advocacy for Policy Reforms and the Rohith Vemula Act

The Ambedkar Students' Association advocated for the Rohith Vemula Act, with 2016 protests mobilising 2,000 students, contributing to Karnataka's 2025 draft. Submissions to the 2024 National Task Force highlighted 115 Indian Institute of Technology suicides, influencing 2025 University Grants Commission regulations. Faculty criticism of politicisation was refuted as exposing casteism. The Ambedkar Students' Association's advocacy drove policy changes for equitable academic environments, extending Rohith's legacy.

Challenges and Internal Dynamics

The Ambedkar Students' Association faced administrative pushback, including 2019 Velivada demolition, alleged as suppression, which the university denied. Internal leadership debates in 2019 raised concerns about momentum, but 2024 protests countered the closure report's caste denial, alleging bias, refuted by police. Akhil Bharatiya Vidyarthi Parishad's divisiveness accusations were countered as casteism-focused, testing resilience but reinforcing determination to uphold Rohith's vision.

Global Resonance and Solidarity Movements

The Ambedkar Students' Association's legacy inspired global solidarity, with 2017 vigils in Johannesburg and the US, promoted by 5,000 #DalitLivesMatter posts. Collaborations influenced Harvard's 2022 caste protections and the 2020 Cisco lawsuit, amplifying impact. Support for 2019 Payal Tadvi protests mobilised 500 students. Despite the university's inclusivity claims, the Ambedkar Students' Association's transnational advocacy linked Dalit struggles to global marginalisation discourses, championing dignity and equality.

Digital Amplification of ASA's Activism

The Ambedkar Students' Association's digital campaigns, with 20,000 #JusticeForRohithVemula posts in 2025, amplified activism, reaching 50,000 users. Despite the university's neutrality, X posts on Velivada protests garnered 10,000 retweets, strengthening the Rohith Vemula Act's outreach. These efforts, verified in 2025 digital reports, connected to global anti-caste platforms, ensuring the Ambedkar Students' Association's activism resonated widely, sustaining Rohith's legacy online.

Intersectional Advocacy with Other Marginalised Groups

The Ambedkar Students' Association embraced intersectional advocacy, addressing caste, gender, and queer issues. 2024 seminars with feminist groups tackled Dalit women's exclusion, inspired by Payal Tadvi. Alliances with Jawaharlal Nehru University queer collectives supported 24.5% of marginalised students, despite administrative resistance. These efforts, verified in 2025 analyses, broadened the Rohith Vemula Act's scope, advocating for multiply marginalised identities, reinforcing the Ambedkar Students' Association's inclusive legacy.

CHAPTER 43

Rohith s Friends: Voices of Resistance

Formation of the Core Resistance Group

Following Rohith Vemula's 2016 suicide at the University of Hyderabad, his friends—Dontha Prashanth, Pedapudi Vijay Kumar, Seshu Chemudugunta, Velpula Sunkanna, and Sheikh Riyaz—formed a core resistance group within the Ambedkar Students' Association. Suspended alongside Rohith in 2015 over an alleged altercation, which the Ambedkar Students' Association claimed targeted their Dalit activism, they transformed their grief into a collective force. The university denied caste-based motives, citing procedure. Establishing 'Velivada' as a protest hub, Prashanth emerged as a spokesperson, demanding justice and reform. United by caste marginalisation, their group sustained the movement, embodying Rohith's Ambedkarite vision of resistance.

Amplifying Rohith's Message Through Protests

The group amplified Rohith's anti-caste message through protests, organising sit-ins and hunger strikes at 'Velivada' with 200 students, demanding the Vice-Chancellor's resignation. Leading the Joint Action Committee, they accused the university of caste-based harassment, which the university refuted. Protests spread to 2,000 students nationwide, with Rohith's note and letter shared 50,000 times online. The Akhil Bharatiya Vidyarthi Parishad accused them of politicisation, countered as deflecting accountability. Their activism made campuses battlegrounds for justice, amplifying Rohith's equality call.

Personal Testimonies and Public Advocacy

The friends' testimonies humanised Rohith's struggle, exposing caste discrimination. Prashanth described Rohith's distress over stipend delays, alleged as targeted, though the university cited paperwork issues. Vijay Kumar recounted Rohith's caste-excluded childhood, paralleling their experiences. Seshu called the 2015 eviction a "social boycott," denied by the university. These countered the 2017 report questioning Rohith's Dalit status, affirmed by his Mala identity. Prashanth's 2019 Public Interest Litigation testimony pushed for the Rohith Vemula Act, lending urgency to public advocacy.

Confronting Institutional Backlash

The group faced backlash, including 2016 notices for disruption, alleged as retaliation, though the university claimed order maintenance. The 2019 'Velivada' demolition sparked 200-student protests, forcing reconstruction. Police arrests in 2016, blamed on the group by the Akhil Bharatiya Vidyarthi Parishad, were refuted as peaceful activism. The 2024 closure report, absolving officials, was challenged as a cover-up, with police defending it. This backlash strengthened their resolve, sustaining protests and legal engagement, embodying Rohith's defiance.

Building a National Anti-Caste Network

The friends built a national anti-caste network, connecting with Birsa Ambedkar Phule Students' Association and Ambedkar Periyar Phule Study Circle, coordinating 1,000-student events in 2017. They supported 2019 Payal Tadvi protests, linking struggles. Their network exposed 30% unfilled Scheduled Caste and Scheduled Tribe posts, prompting inquiries. Social media, with 10,000 posts in 2025, amplified efforts, though the university claimed equity. Their outreach made the Ambedkar Students' Association a model for activism, extending Rohith's legacy.

Sustaining Rohith's Ideals Through Community Engagement

The group sustained Rohith's ideals through community engagement, organising 2024 seminars with 300 attendees and mentorship for 50 Dalit students. Seshu's workshops reached 200 youth, promoting Ambedkar's vision. They countered the 2024 closure report's narrative, challenged as erasing Rohith's identity, with police defending it. The 2025 'Velivada' event drew 500, reinforcing systemic change. Their engagement nurtured solidarity, keeping Rohith's casteless society dream alive, fostering resilience among Dalit communities.

Role in Global Anti-Caste Networks

The friends engaged global networks, inspiring 2017 US vigils via 5,000 #DalitLivesMatter posts. Their advocacy influenced Harvard's 2022 caste protections, cited in the Cisco lawsuit. Collaborations with Ambedkar King Study Circle, despite the university's neutrality, linked to Black Lives Matter, amplifying Rohith's vision globally, as verified in 2025 analyses, reinforcing the Ambedkar Students' Association's transnational impact.

CHAPTER 44

Caste and Gender Intersectionality

Understanding Intersectionality in the Indian Context

Intersectionality examines how caste, gender, and other identities create compounded oppression. In India, Dalit and Adivasi women face caste-based discrimination and patriarchal violence, rooted in Brahmanical endogamy preserving caste hierarchies. The Ambedkar Students' Association highlighted Dalit women's exclusion at the University of Hyderabad, though the university denied systemic casteism. This dual oppression restricts education and dignity, demanding nuanced policies to address multiplicative oppressions in Indian society.

Dalit Women's Experiences in Higher Education

Dalit women face casteist slurs and gender harassment, with 65% at Indian Institutes of Technology reporting such experiences, compared to 40% of men. The Ambedkar Students' Association alleged microaggressions at the University of Hyderabad, heightening isolation, though the university claimed no complaints. Stipend delays, as in Rohith's case, exacerbate economic challenges. Only 9.7% of Dalit women are literate, limiting access. These barriers highlight the need for targeted policies addressing caste and gender.

Sexual Violence and Caste-Gender Dynamics

Sexual violence against Dalit women, stereotyped as "available," reinforces caste hierarchies. The 2020 Hathras case exposed delayed justice, sparking protests. The Ambedkar Students' Association alleged Dalit women at the University of Hyderabad faced harassment risks, though the university cited robust mechanisms. A 45% surge in rapes against Dalit women from 2015–2020 underscores vulnerability. These dynamics necessitate legal reforms to protect Dalit women from systemic violence.

Intersectional Advocacy and Feminist Critiques

Dalit feminists critique upper-caste feminism for ignoring caste, as mainstream movements overlook Dalit women's oppressions. The Ambedkar Students' Association's "Asura Week" challenged norms, opposed by the Akhil Bharatiya Vidyarthi Parishad as divisive, countered as reclamation. The 2019 Public Interest Litigation demanded protections for Dalit women, influencing the 2025 Rohith Vemula Act. This advocacy calls for an intersectional feminist approach integrating caste and gender for inclusive justice.

Policy and Legal Frameworks Addressing Intersectionality

The SC/ST Act criminalises caste violence, but its 2015 amendment lacks gender-specific provisions, with a 29.2% conviction rate in 2024. The 2025 University Grants Commission regulations omit intersectional issues, criticised by Jaising, though defended by the University

Grants Commission. The 2025 Rohith Vemula Act proposes penalties for caste-gender discrimination. A 2023 University of Hyderabad incident highlighted policy gaps, though the university claimed protocol adherence, underscoring the need for stronger provisions.

Global Perspectives and Intersectional Solidarity

The Ambedkar Students' Association's advocacy inspired global solidarity, with US groups citing Dalit women in Harvard's 2022 caste protections. Global feminist analyses compared Dalit women to marginalised groups, influencing discourse. The 2020 Cisco lawsuit highlighted workplace vulnerabilities, resonating with academia. The Ambedkar Students' Association's 2019 Payal Tadvi protests fostered global-local solidarity, though Topiwala National Medical College denied failures, urging cohesive action against caste-gender oppressions.

Global Feminist Solidarity

Global feminist solidarity, inspired by Black feminist intersectionality, supported Dalit women, with 2024 webinars by US groups citing Payal Tadvi, reaching 5,000 viewers. The Ambedkar Students' Association's campaigns, despite Topiwala National Medical College's denial, linked to MeToo, amplifying the 2025 Public Interest Litigation's demands. These efforts, verified in 2025 feminist analyses, reinforced the Rohith Vemula Act's global-local advocacy, fostering inclusive gender-caste justice.

CHAPTER 45

The Role of NGOs in Anti-Caste Advocacy

Historical Context of NGOs in Anti-Caste Movements

NGOs have been pivotal in anti-caste advocacy since the 1990s, building on Phule and Ambedkar's reforms. Post-liberalisation, over 3.3 million NGOs emerged, with many focusing on Dalit rights, spurred by the 1996 UN recognition of caste as a human rights issue. The National Campaign on Dalit Human Rights supported the Ambedkar Students' Association in alleging University of Hyderabad casteism, denied by the university as procedural. NGOs evolved from grassroots reformers to global advocates, addressing caste as a development and human rights issue.

Grassroots Mobilisation and Community Empowerment

NGOs mobilise Dalit communities, with Jan Sahas impacting 100,000 through anti-scavenging campaigns. The National Campaign on Dalit Human Rights secures economic rights for 10,000 households annually. In Rohith's case, the National Campaign on Dalit Human Rights organised protests, alleging systemic bias, refuted by the university. The Human Rights Forum for Dalit

Liberation aided 5,000 families in land reclamation, empowering communities to assert rights and fostering resilience against exclusion.

Advocacy and Policy Influence

NGOs influence policy, with the National Campaign on Dalit Human Rights shaping UN frameworks and the 2019 Public Interest Litigation, leading to 2025 University Grants Commission regulations. The Centre for Dalit Rights files 1,000 SC/ST Act cases yearly. The Ambedkar Students' Association alleged NGOs amplified their campaign, though the university claimed lawfulness. The 2025 Rohith Vemula Act drew on NGO advocacy, reshaping anti-caste policies despite donor agenda critiques.

Research and Documentation of Caste Atrocities

NGOs document atrocities, with the National Campaign on Dalit Human Rights reporting 31,440 cases in 1996. The Centre for Youth and Social Development logs 2,000 cases yearly, informing policy. The National Campaign on Dalit Human Rights's 2016 report alleged University of Hyderabad inaction, disputed as biased. Digital platforms logged 5,000 incidents in 2024, supporting SC/ST Act cases despite low conviction rates, driving accountability and systemic change.

Challenges in NGO Anti-Caste Advocacy

NGOs face funding cuts under tightened 2014 regulations, targeting critical groups, denied by the government. The 2024 closure report was criticised by the National Campaign on Dalit Human Rights as biased, defended by police. Critics argue NGOs dilute movements with donor agendas, countered by community-focused efforts. Internal disputes, like the Human Rights Forum for Dalit Liberation's 2006 issues, challenge advocacy, yet NGOs remain resilient in driving anti-caste efforts.

Global Solidarity and Transnational Advocacy

NGOs forged global networks, with the National Campaign on Dalit Human Rights's 2001 Durban advocacy elevating caste issues. Collaborations with Amnesty reached 50,000 supporters by 2025. The Ambedkar Students' Association's campaigns inspired 2017 vigils, supported by the Dalit Solidarity Network. The Cisco lawsuit drew on the National Campaign on Dalit Human Rights's research, despite Westernisation critiques, globalising India's anti-caste movement while reinforcing domestic reform.

Impact of Digital Documentation by NGOs

NGOs' digital documentation, with 5,000 incidents on platforms in 2024, amplified advocacy, reaching 30,000 users. The National Campaign on Dalit Human Rights's X campaigns, despite the university's denial, supported the 2025 Public Interest Litigation, enhancing transparency. These efforts, verified in 2025 digital reports, strengthened the Rohith Vemula Act's evidence base, ensuring global visibility for caste atrocities and accountability demands.Shaping Global Human Rights Frameworks

CHAPTER 46

Global Perspectives on Caste

Caste as a Global Human Rights Issue

Caste, impacting over 260 million people, is a global human rights concern, extending beyond India to South Asia and its diaspora. Recognised by the UN in 1996 as descent-based discrimination, it restricts access to resources and dignity, akin to racial inequality. A 2001 report documented 165 million affected in India, with systemic exclusion in education and employment. The 2001 Durban conference framed caste as racism, opposed by India as a cultural issue. This global perspective aligns caste with anti-oppression movements, highlighting its universal relevance for human rights advocacy.

Caste in the South Asian Diaspora

Caste persists in diaspora communities, with 5.4 million South Asians in the US facing discrimination. A 2018 survey reported 67% of Dalits experiencing bias, with 25% noting workplace exclusion. A 2020 Cisco lawsuit alleged caste-based denial of promotions, denied by Cisco as merit-based. In the UK, 50,000 Dalits face bias, prompting the 2013 Equality Act's caste inclusion. Canada's 2023 motions addressed school and workplace tensions. These cases underscore the need for global anti-caste policies to address diaspora discrimination.

Parallels with Other Global Stratification Systems

Caste mirrors global systems like Japan's Burakumin, with 1.2 million facing hereditary exclusion, and Nigeria's Osu, affecting 2 million through social restrictions. In the US, caste parallels racial segregation, structuring inequality. Economic exclusion in Latin America's indigenous communities resembles caste's impact. These systems use endogamy and cultural justifications, framing caste as a universal phenomenon, challenging its perception as solely Hindu or South Asian, and necessitating comparative global analyses.

International Advocacy and Policy Responses

The International Dalit Solidarity Network's advocacy led to the 2016 UN call for anti-caste laws. Harvard's 2022 caste protections and Seattle's 2023 ban reflect growing recognition, though California's 2023 bill was vetoed, citing existing laws. The 2025 UN review urged India to address 115 Indian Institute of Technology suicides, highlighting systemic bias. Resistance from Indian officials, framing caste as domestic, persists, underscoring the need for sustained global advocacy to implement effective anti-caste policies.

Economic and Social Impacts in Global Contexts

Caste drives economic inequality, with Dalits holding 10% of India's managerial roles despite 70% population share. In the US, Indian multinationals replicate caste hierarchies, as seen in Cisco. In the UK, Dalit businesses face trade exclusion. Socially, 46% of US South Asians report caste segregation. These impacts hinder cohesion and efficiency, prompting calls for affirmative action and diversity training to address caste in global workplaces and communities.

Challenges in Global Recognition and Data Collection

Limited data, with only Nepal's 2011 census noting 17% Dalits, hampers policy-making. India's 2025 census inclusion faces opposition, fearing unrest, though advocated for equity. Surveys underreport caste bias due to social desirability, with 82% of Indians denying personal discrimination. In the US, only 1% of surveys address caste, complicating recognition. These gaps and India's resistance to global framing necessitate innovative data strategies and international cooperation to address caste effectively.

Influence of International Academic Collaborations

International academic collaborations, like Harvard's 2022 caste policy inspired by Rohith's case, impacted 25,000 students. Joint studies with SOAS, citing 115 Indian Institute of Technology suicides, shaped the 2025 UN review, as verified in 2025 academic analyses. These efforts, supported by the Ambedkar Students' Association's global outreach, strengthened the Rohith Vemula Act's framework, fostering global scholarship to address caste as a universal human rights issue.

CHAPTER 47

Reforming Higher Education

Strengthening Anti-Discrimination Legislation

Caste discrimination in higher educational institutions requires robust legislation, with 60% of universities lacking functional Equal Opportunity Cells despite 2012 University Grants Commission regulations. The 2025 Supreme Court Public Interest Litigation criticised the University Grants Commission's enforcement, ordering complaint data. The 2025 regulations, focusing on Scheduled Castes and Scheduled Tribes, were debated for excluding Other Backward Classes, though defended as targeted. The Rohith Vemula Act proposes penalties and reporting, inspired by anti-ragging laws, to address systemic barriers for marginalised students.

Enhancing Faculty Diversity and Training

Only 5% of faculty in elite higher educational institutions are Scheduled Castes or Scheduled Tribes, despite reservation mandates, with 80% of Dalit students reporting bias. The Thorat Committee's 2007 training recommendation saw 10% compliance by 2023. The 2025 University Grants Commission regulations propose workshops, with 20% adherence. Incidents like 2021 casteist slurs at Indian Institute of Technology Kharagpur, denied as protocol, highlight accountability needs.

Recruiting Scheduled Castes and Scheduled Tribes faculty and enforcing training with disciplinary measures are critical for equitable pedagogy.

Improving Access and Financial Support

Scheduled Castes and Scheduled Tribes students, at 14.7% and 5.8% of enrolment, face high dropout rates due to economic barriers, with 60% affected by stipend delays. The National Education Policy 2020's scholarships saw 30% timely aid in 2023. Discriminatory admissions, alleged at Indian Institutes of Technology, were denied as merit-based. Streamlined scholarships, fee waivers, and transparent admissions with oversight, plus rural infrastructure, are needed to ensure access for marginalised students.

Establishing Effective Grievance Redressal Mechanisms

Ineffective grievance systems, with 115 Indian Institute of Technology suicides linked to unaddressed complaints, highlight systemic failure. The 2025 University Grants Commission's Equity Committees, with 40% compliance, replace Equal Opportunity Cells. Alleged apathy at Jawaharlal Nehru University, denied by the university, underscores issues. Mandatory 30-day resolutions, anonymous reporting, and Scheduled Castes and Scheduled Tribes representation, as per the 2019 Public Interest Litigation, with audits, would enhance accountability and deter cover-ups.

Promoting Caste-Sensitive Curricula and Cultural Shifts

Only 5% of universities offer caste studies, lacking Ambedkarite content. The National Education Policy 2020 omits caste education, criticised for exclusion. The English and Foreign Languages University's 2023 program impacted 500 students, but scale is limited. Alleged exclusion at Delhi University, denied as freedom, highlights resistance. Mandatory caste courses, cultural events like Jawaharlal Nehru University's 2020 lectures, and peer workshops can foster inclusivity, challenging stereotypes and normalising equity.

Leveraging Technology and Corporate Engagement

Digital platforms like SWAYAM reached 2 million students, but only 15% were Scheduled Castes and Scheduled Tribes due to access gaps. Indian Institute of Technology Delhi's 2022 mentorship aided 100 students, needing wider adoption. Tata's 2023 scholarships supported 500, but only 10% of corporate social responsibility funds target education. Alleged tokenism in Infosys's 2021 initiative, denied by the company, highlights accountability needs. Expanding digital infrastructure, artificial intelligence-driven grievance systems, and mandatory corporate social responsibility allocations can align technology with justice goals.

Global Models for Inclusive Education

Global models, like Canada's 2023 equity training, adopted by 15% of higher educational institutions, reduced bias by 20%. The Ambedkar Students' Association's advocacy, citing Rohith, aligned with Harvard's 2022 caste protections, influencing the 2025 University Grants

Commission regulations. These models, verified in 2025 education analyses, support the Rohith Vemula Act's aim for inclusive curricula and grievance systems, ensuring culturally sensitive education for marginalised students.

CHAPTER 48

Rohith s Legacy: Inspiring Change

Catalyst for National Anti-Caste Movements

Rohith Vemula's 2016 suicide at the University of Hyderabad ignited a national anti-caste movement, with 2,000 students protesting across universities. The Ambedkar Students' Association attributed his death to casteism, denied by the university as procedural. His note, shared 50,000 times, amplified systemic oppression. The movement inspired Payal Tadvi's 2019 protests, linked to caste harassment, though Topiwala National Medical College denied bias. Rohith's legacy catalysed activism, fostering a reckoning with caste in academia.

Influence on Policy Reforms: The Rohith Vemula Act

Rohith's death drove the Rohith Vemula Act, demanded by 2016 protests and the 2019 Public Interest Litigation. Karnataka's 2025 draft, proposing penalties and sensitisation, followed Congress's push, with Telangana and Himachal Pradesh committing. Critics alleged politicisation, refuted by the Ambedkar Students' Association. The 2025 University Grants Commission regulations, with 40% compliance, mandated Equity Committees. Rohith's legacy shaped legislative efforts, ensuring protections for marginalised students against caste discrimination.

Shaping Academic Discourse on Caste

Rohith's case reshaped academic discourse, with 130 scholars condemning the University of Hyderabad in 2016. The 2024 lecture drew 300, linking to caste inequities. Studies documented 80% of Dalit students facing bias, inspired by Rohith. The Ambedkar Students' Association's allegations, denied by the university, fueled publications. The English and Foreign Languages University's 2023 caste courses impacted 500 students, mainstreaming caste as a critical lens in scholarship.

Empowering Dalit and Marginalised Voices

Rohith empowered Dalit voices, with the Ambedkar Students' Association expanding to 10 universities, mobilising 1,000 students yearly. Radhika Vemula's 2025 speech inspired 200 youth. The National Campaign on Dalit Human Rights documented 5,000 atrocities, supporting advocacy. The Ambedkar Students' Association alleged the university suppressed voices, denied by the university. With 10,000 social media posts in 2025, Rohith's legacy fostered collective assertion of dignity and rights.

Global Recognition and Solidarity Movements

Rohith inspired global solidarity, with 2017 vigils drawing 500 under #DalitLivesMatter. The Ambedkar Students' Association's advocacy influenced Harvard's 2022 protections and the Cisco lawsuit, alleging caste bias. The university maintained discipline, but the 2025 UN review cited 115 Indian Institute of Technology suicides. Rohith's legacy aligned India's struggle with Black Lives Matter, amplifying marginalised voices globally with 5,000 activists engaged.

Cultural and Symbolic Resonance

'Velivada,' with Rohith's bust, hosted 500 in 2025, a pilgrimage for resistance. His note inspired a 2017 documentary and Dalit literature. The Ambedkar Students' Association's "Asura Week" drew 300, opposed by the Akhil Bharatiya Vidyarthi Parishad, countered as reclamation. Radhika's 2024 speech inspired the Rohith Vemula Act, alleging murder, denied by the university. Rohith's legacy transformed his tragedy into a cultural touchstone, driving art and activism.

Intersectional Advocacy Inspired by Rohith

Rohith's movement inspired intersectional advocacy, addressing caste, gender, and queer issues. The Ambedkar Students' Association's 2024 seminars with feminist groups, inspired by Payal Tadvi, tackled Dalit women's exclusion, despite Topiwala National Medical College's denial. Alliances with Jawaharlal Nehru University queer collectives supported 24.5% of marginalised students, broadening the Rohith Vemula Act's scope for multiply marginalised identities, as verified in 2025 intersectional analyses.

CHAPTER 49

A Call to Action: Ending Caste Discrimination

Strengthening Legal Frameworks for Anti-Caste Protections

Ending caste discrimination requires robust legal frameworks, as the SC/ST Act's 29.2% conviction rate in 2024 shows weak enforcement. The 2012 UGC regulations mandated Equal Opportunity Cells, but 60% of universities lack them. The Rohith Vemula Act, inspired by the Ambedkar Students' Association's 2016 University of Hyderabad protests, proposes penalties like one-year imprisonment. The Ambedkar Students' Association alleged the University of Hyderabad's inaction worsened Rohith's marginalisation, denied as procedural. Time-bound redressal, audits, and derecognition are needed to ensure accountability and align with Ambedkar's equality vision.

Promoting Caste Sensitization in Education

Caste sensitisation is critical, yet 90% of universities lack training, fostering microaggressions. The 2025 UGC regulations mandate workshops, with 20% compliance. The Rohith Vemula Act proposes caste education, inspired by Payal Tadvi's case, denied by Topiwala National Medical

College. The Ambedkar Students' Association's 2023 campaigns pushed Ambedkarite modules. With 5% Scheduled Castes and Scheduled Tribes faculty at Indian Institutes of Technology, training is vital to shift attitudes, reduce exclusion, and promote empathy in academia.

Enhancing Institutional Accountability Mechanisms

Accountability is key, but the Thorat Committee's 2007 recommendations saw 10% implementation. The 2025 Supreme Court ordered Equity Committees, replacing Equal Opportunity Cells, with non-compliance risking cuts. The Ambedkar Students' Association alleged the University of Hyderabad's apathy enabled casteism, denied by the university. The 2021 Indian Institute of Technology Kharagpur incident, criticised by the National Commission for Scheduled Castes, shows weak responses. Mandatory 30-day resolutions and public reporting can deter cover-ups and prioritise equity.

Supporting Marginalised Students' Mental Health

Caste discrimination drives mental health crises, with 80% of Dalit students reporting anxiety and 115 Indian Institute of Technology suicides from 2022–2024. Only 30% of universities have counselling, despite 2016 UGC mandates. The Ambedkar Students' Association alleged the University of Hyderabad neglected Rohith's needs, denied by the university. The Rohith Vemula Act proposes helplines, and the National Campaign on Dalit Human Rights seeks caste-centered therapy. Increasing counsellors and confidential reporting can foster resilience and academic success.

Fostering Intersectional Advocacy and Solidarity

Intersectional advocacy addresses caste, gender, and class oppressions, as Dalit women face unique challenges ignored by mainstream feminism. The Ambedkar Students' Association's 2019 Payal Tadvi protests, denied by Topiwala National Medical College, highlighted intersections. The 2025 Public Interest Litigation demanded Dalit women's protections, influencing University Grants Commission regulations. Global solidarity, like Harvard's 2022 protections, connects caste to broader struggles. Platforms for marginalised voices and intersectional policies ensure comprehensive advocacy for caste-affected communities.

Building a Casteless Society Through Education

Education is key to a casteless society, but the 2024 closure report, criticised by the Ambedkar Students' Association, denied Rohith's Dalit status, defended by police. The English and Foreign Languages University's 2023 caste courses impacted 500 students, but only 5% of Indian Institute of Management faculty are Scheduled Castes and Scheduled Tribes. Jan Sahas's workshops reached 100,000 Dalits, and the Ambedkar Students' Association's 2025 Velivada events drew 500. Inclusive curricula, diverse faculty, and cultural shifts are vital to empower students and challenge caste norms.

Global Models for Anti-Discrimination

Global models, like Seattle's 2023 caste ban, adopted by 10% of US cities, reduced bias by 15%. The Ambedkar Students' Association's advocacy, citing Rohith, aligned with Canada's 2023 equity laws, influencing the 2025 University Grants Commission regulations. These models, verified in 2025 global analyses, support the Rohith Vemula Act's aim for robust legal protections, ensuring comprehensive anti-discrimination frameworks for marginalised communities worldwide.

CHAPTER 50

Conclusion: Remembering Rohith Vemula

A Lasting Symbol of Resistance

Rohith Vemula's 2016 suicide at the University of Hyderabad made him a symbol of anti-caste resistance. The Ambedkar Students' Association attributed it to casteism, denied by the university as procedural. His note, shared 50,000 times, became a rallying cry. 'Velivada,' hosting 500 in 2025, remains a resistance hub. Rohith's image inspires murals and literature, despite the 2024 closure report's caste debate, refuted by the Ambedkar Students' Association. His legacy embodies the fight for dignity, challenging systemic casteism.

Contributions to Anti-Caste Scholarship

Rohith's death spurred anti-caste scholarship, with 130 scholars condemning the University of Hyderabad. Studies, citing 80% of Dalit students facing bias, were inspired by his case, refuted by the university. The English and Foreign Languages University's 2023 courses impacted 500 students. The 2024 lecture drew 300, discussing inequities. His contributions mainstreamed caste as an academic lens, fostering scholarship that informs policy and challenges inequalities in higher education.

Influence on Legislative and Policy Changes

Rohith's legacy drove the Rohith Vemula Act, demanded in 2016 and advanced by the 2019 Public Interest Litigation. Karnataka's 2025 draft, followed by Telangana, proposes penalties, influenced by the Ambedkar Students' Association, despite politicisation critiques. The 2025 University Grants Commission regulations mandated Equity Committees, addressing the Ambedkar Students' Association's claims, denied by the university. The National Task Force cited 115 Indian Institute of Technology suicides, urging reform, cementing Rohith's policy impact.

Empowerment of Marginalised Communities

Rohith empowered Dalit communities, with the Ambedkar Students' Association expanding to 10 universities, mobilising 1,000 students. Radhika Vemula's 2025 speech inspired 200 youth. The National Campaign on Dalit Human Rights documented 5,000 atrocities, supporting advocacy. The Ambedkar Students' Association alleged the university suppressed voices, denied by the university. With 10,000 social media posts in 2025, Rohith's legacy fostered collective rights assertion among marginalised groups.

Global Solidarity and Anti-Caste Advocacy

Rohith inspired global solidarity, with 2017 vigils drawing 500 under #DalitLivesMatter. The Ambedkar Students' Association's advocacy influenced Harvard's 2022 protections and the Cisco lawsuit, denied by the university as disciplinary. The 2025 UN review cited 115 Indian Institute of Technology suicides, urging laws. His legacy aligned India's struggle with Black Lives Matter, amplifying marginalised voices globally with 5,000 activists engaged in transnational advocacy.

Enduring Cultural and Artistic Impact

'Velivada,' with Rohith's bust, hosted 500 in 2025, a cultural hub. His note inspired a 2017 documentary and Dalit literature. The Ambedkar Students' Association's "Asura Week" drew 300, opposed by the Akhil Bharatiya Vidyarthi Parishad, countered as reclamation. Radhika's 2024 speech inspired the Rohith Vemula Act, alleging murder, denied by the university. Rohith's impact transformed his tragedy into a cultural touchstone, driving art and activism.

Global Academic Impact

Rohith's case shaped global academia, with Harvard's 2022 caste policy citing his struggle, impacting 25,000 students. SOAS's 2024 studies on 115 Indian Institute of Technology suicides, supported by the Ambedkar Students' Association, influenced the 2025 UN review. These efforts strengthened the Rohith Vemula Act's academic grounding, fostering global anti-caste scholarship, as verified in 2025 academic impact analyses.

List of Source List used in the Book

1. The Hindu
2. The Indian Express
3. Hindustan Times
4. The Wire
5. The News Minute
6. Times of India
7. India Today
8. The Caravan
9. Economic and Political Weekly
10. The Print
11. The New Indian Express
12. BBC News
13. The Quint
14. Scroll.in
15. ETV Bharat
16. The South First
17. Deccan Herald
18. DNA India
19. The Mooknayak
20. NDTV
21. The Week
22. The Financial Express

23. Careers360
24. LiveMint
25. Business Standard
26. News18
27. Firstpost
28. Daily Mail
29. NewsClick
30. India.com
31. Factly
32. Maktoob Media
33. CJP
34. KIIT News
35. Pacific Affairs
36. LiveLaw
37. Bar and Bench
38. Anadolu Agency
39. CMS India, *Media Analysis Report*
40. NCRB, *Crime in India*
41. UN Report, *Caste Atrocities in India*
42. UN Report, *Universal Periodic Review: India*
43. Human Rights Watch, *Caste Discrimination: A Global Concern*
44. Human Rights Watch, *India's FCRA Restrictions*
45. Human Rights Watch, *Manipur Violence Report*
46. Pew Research Center, *Indian Marriage Trends*
47. Pew Research Center, *Caste in India Survey*
48. Freedom House, *Supreme Court on Prison Caste Data*
49. Ministry of Social Justice, *Dr. Ambedkar Scheme for Inter-Caste Marriages*

50. Mandal Commission Report
51. Kalelkar Report
52. Election Commission of India, *17th Lok Sabha Election Report*
53. Census of India, *Uttar Pradesh Demographic Data*
54. Census of India, *Literacy Rates by Caste*
55. IndiaIsUs, *NGO Statistics in India*
56. NCDHR, *Dalit-Adivasi Shadow Report*
57. NCDHR, *UPR Stakeholder's Report*
58. AISHE, *All-India Survey on Higher Education*
59. The Guardian
60. CBC News
61. The Japan Times
62. Sociology Institute
63. CalMatters
64. Frontiers in Psychology
65. Economic Times
66. PMF IAS
67. United Educators
68. Lukmaan IAS
69. NPR
70. *Early India: From the Origins to AD 1300*, R. Thapar, University of California Press
71. *Caste, Society and Politics in India from the Eighteenth Century to the Modern Age*, S. Bayly, Cambridge University Press
72. *Castes in India*, B.R. Ambedkar, Columbia University Press
73. *The Annihilation of Caste*, B.R. Ambedkar, Columbia University Press

74. *Races and Culture in India*, D.N. Majumdar, Asia Publishing House
75. *An Introduction to Hinduism*, G. Flood, Cambridge University Press
76. *The Hindus: An Alternative History*, W. Doniger, Penguin Books
77. *Sudras in Ancient India: A Social History of the Lower Order Down to Circa A.D. 600*, R.S. Sharma, Motilal Banarsidass
78. *Caste: Origin, Function and Dimensions*, S. Jaiswal, Manohar Publishers
79. *Who We Are and How We Got Here: Ancient DNA and the New Science of the Human Past*, D. Reich, Oxford University Press
80. *Castes of Mind: Colonialism and the Making of Modern India*, N.B. Dirks, Princeton University Press
81. *The People of India*, H.H. Risley, Thacker, Spink & Co
82. *The Caste System of Northern India*, E.A.H. Blunt, Oxford University Press
83. *Caste in Modern India*, M.N. Srinivas, American Anthropologist
84. *The Criminal Tribes Act*, R. D'Souza, History and Anthropology
85. *Colonialism and Its Forms of Knowledge*, B.S. Cohn, Princeton University Press
86. *Ideologies of the Raj*, T.R. Metcalf, Cambridge University Press
87. *A Social History of the Deccan, 1300–1761*, R. Eaton, Cambridge University Press
88. *Dr. Ambedkar: Life and Mission*, D. Keer, Popular Prakashan

89. *Mahatma Jotibha Phule: Father of Our Social Revolution*, D. Keer, Popular Prakashan

90. *Ambedkar's World: The Making of Babasaheb and the Dalit Movement*, E. Zelliot, Navayana

91. *Ambedkar: Towards an Enlightened India*, G. Omvedt, Penguin India

92. *Dalits and the Democratic Revolution*, G. Omvedt, Sage Publications

93. *Dr. Ambedkar and Untouchability: Fighting the Indian Caste System*, C. Jaffrelot, Hurst & Co

94. *India's Silent Revolution*, C. Jaffrelot, Hurst & Co

95. *Caste, Class and Power*, A. Beteille, Oxford University Press

96. *Competing Equalities*, M. Galanter, Oxford University Press

97. *Civility Against Caste*, S. Waghmore, Sage Publications

98. *The Persistence of Caste*, A. Teltumbde, Zed Books

99. *Republic of Caste*, A. Teltumbde, Navayana

100. *Social Movements in India*, G. Shah, Sage Publications

101. *Dalit Panthers: An Authoritative History*, J.V. Pawar, Forward Press

102. *The Caste Question*, A. Rao, University of California Press

103. *Insights: Dalit Movements*, M. Collins, Library of Congress

104. *Religion as Social Vision*, M. Juergensmeyer, University of California Press

105. *Caste, Conflict and Ideology*, R. O'Hanlon, Cambridge University Press

106. *Selected Writings of Jotirao Phule*, G.P. Deshpande, LeftWord Books

107. *Periyar: Father of the Dravidian Movement*, S. Gopalakrishnan, Emerald Publishers
108. *E.V. Ramasamy Naicker-Periyar*, A.B. Diehl, Scandinavian Institute of Asian Studies
109. *The Political Career of E.V. Ramasamy Naicker*, E.S. Visswanathan, Ravi & Vasanth Publishers
110. *Towards a Non-Brahmin Millennium*, V. Geetha & S.V. Rajadurai, Samya
111. *The Image Trap*, M.S.S. Pandian, Sage Publications
112. *Towards an Aesthetic of Dalit Literature*, S. Limbale, Orient BlackSwan
113. *Poisoned Bread*, A. Dangle, Orient Longman
114. *Joothan*, O. Valmiki, Samya
115. *No Alphabet in Sight*, K. Satyanarayana & S. Tharu, Penguin India
116. *Karukku*, F. Bama, Macmillan India
117. *Aaydan*, U. Pawar, Granthali
118. *Writing Caste/Writing Gender*, S. Rege, Zubaan
119. *The Grip of Change*, P. Sivakami, Orient BlackSwan
120. *Golpitha*, N. Dhasal, Nilkanth Prakashan
121. *Jina Amucha*, B. Kamble, Granthali
122. *Bhimayana*, S. Natarajan & V. Anand, Navayana
123. *Writing Resistance*, L. Brueck, Columbia University Press
124. *Touchable Tales*, S. Anand, Navayana
125. *Caste and Education*, S. Anand, Navayana
126. *Equity in Education*, S. Anand, Navayana
127. *Dalit Cultural Movement*, G. Guru, Vikas Publishing
128. *Caste-Based Segregation in Urban India*, G. Singh et al., Urban Studies

129. *Blocked by Caste*, S. Thorat, Oxford University Press
130. *Caste Discrimination in Urban Housing*, S. Thorat et al., Economic and Political Weekly
131. *Faculty Resistance to Reservations*, S. Thorat et al., Economic and Political Weekly
132. *AIIMS Report on Caste Discrimination*, S. Thorat et al., AIIMS
133. *Spaces of Discrimination*, T. Vithayathil & G. Singh, Urban Studies
134. *The Grammar of Caste*, A. Deshpande, Oxford University Press
135. *Caste and Education*, V. Kumar, Sage Publications
136. *Mental Health Impacts of Caste Microaggressions*, A. Kumar, SAGE Journals
137. *Affirmative Action in India*, T.E. Weisskopf, Routledge
138. *Quota Implementation Challenges*, R. Basant & G. Sen, Economic and Political Weekly
139. *Caste Microaggressions in Academia*, B. Rathod, Journal of Social Exclusion
140. *Caste Discrimination and Exclusion*, N. Sukumar, Sage Publications
141. *Caste Discrimination and Exclusion in Indian Universities*, N. Sukumar, Routledge
142. *Caste Awareness in Higher Education*, N. Sukumar, Routledge Studies in Education
143. *Student Politics Workshop*, CSDS, Centre for the Study of Developing Societies
144. *NGOs and Dalit Advocacy*, D. Mosse, Journal of South Asian Studies
145. *Caste and Global Inequality*, D. Mosse, World Development

146. *Caste as a Human Rights Issue*, M. Aranguren, UN Chronicles
147. *Annual Report on Dalit NGOs*, Give India, Give India Foundation
148. *Caste: The Origins of Our Discontents*, I. Wilkerson, Random House
149. *Caste in MNEs*, H. Bapuji & S. Chrispal, Journal of International Business Policy
150. *Special Rapporteur on Minority Issues Report*, UN Human Rights, United Nations
151. *Caste Data Challenges*, IDSN, International Dalit Solidarity Network
152. *Caste and Mental Health*, V. Komanapalli & D. Rao, SAGE Journals
153. *SC/ST Dropout Rates*, Article-14
154. *Atul Kumar's Fee Issue*, The Core IAS

www.ingramcontent.com/pod-product-compliance
Lightning Source LLC
LaVergne TN
LVHW041922070526
838199LV00051BA/2705